Develop You, Develop Your Team … on the RightPath

Develop You, Develop Your Team ... on the RightPath

ISBN 13: 978-1482731262
ISBN-10: 1482731266

DEDICATION

This book is dedicated with love and appreciation to my wife, Penny Gaultney Mabe, my greatest blessing. She has graciously and lovingly endured my behaviors (and lack thereof!) and my strong "hard-wiring" for 26 years. Thank you for helping to make this vision called RightPath possible.

It is also dedicated to my two other blessings, my son Micah and my daughter Joy who work to keep us young while continually reminding me what family is all about.
I love each of you to the moon and back!

ACKNOWLEDGEMENTS

There is no adequate way to say "thanks" to Terri Hintz, the cornerstone of the RightPath team. Without her help, support and encouragement this book would never have seen the light of day! Also, RightPath could not be where it is today without her.
Thank you, Terri…you're the Best!

I must give special thanks to Sheri McHugh, Jennifer Radak, Nancy Beggs and Lisa Buurman – all a valuable part of the RightPath team as well as our many coaches and facilitators around the globe.

There are so many people who have played a role in growing this vision called RightPath and allowing it to impact people worldwide that I could not begin to name them all. You know who you are and I have tried to say thanks along the way. I appreciate you being part of this vision and am thankful for you being on the RightPath with me!

.

WHAT OTHERS ARE SAYING!

"The Senior Leader Program at Goodwill Industries International is an intense and challenging program we offer to member Goodwill's across the country and Canada. Jerry Mabe and RightPath have been a valuable part of this leadership program since its' inception in 2008. Their tools and curricula provide leaders with powerful insights and information they can immediately put to work in their own Goodwill's."

Susan E. Gabriel, Director of Senior Leadership & Management Programs, Goodwill Industries International

"Many years ago, we set out very intentionally in our organization to develop a culture of on-going personal development, today known as coaching. We sought to empower our leaders, and soon discovered that coaching was paramount to their on-going success and ability to keep pace with the rapid organizational growth. Then, as these senior leaders started to see the results, they took what they had learned and began, in turn, to coach their own team. This belief in helping each other to grow and the coaching culture we have created now define who we are as an organization, as leaders, and as team mates. Jerry Mabe and RightPath have been an integral part of this process and success. Their assessment tools are the solid foundation on which our on-going development is built."

Jane Nichols, CEO, Goodwill Industries of the Southern Rivers

"RightPath has been the instrument that has assisted me, the staff, our launch team, and our church leadership to more deeply know who we are and how we are wired to work together with one another. No other tool is able to create profiles that reveal personal strengths and struggles in a manner that cultivates individual development while also creating an awareness of how those personalized profiles fit with one another in the building of healthy teams. We use RightPath every year in staff and lay leadership development. I could not think of a better investment for a church planter."

Bart Garrett, Planter and Lead Pastor of Christ Church Berkeley

"Our winning strategy includes a focus on developing talent – both on and off the field. No matter the level or role, associates in the Atlanta Falcons organization and the broader Blank Family of Businesses are provided with opportunities to develop their leadership skills and take their performance to the next level. RightPath assessments and Jerry Mabe's coaching have been an important part of our leadership playbook for many years."

Arthur M. Blank, Owner & Chairman, Atlanta Falcons

"Since 2001, RightPath's validated tools have helped us to create a solid foundation to successfully develop our leaders and teams. Jerry Mabe and RightPath have a common understanding of behavior and talent which allows us all to speak the same language developmentally and ensures we have the right people in the right positions. I believe this book will help others to do the same."

Randy Pope, Pastor, Perimeter Church, Atlanta, GA

"I have long known the powerful impact of behavior in leadership and personal development. In his new book, Jerry Mabe, CEO of RightPath, will guide you to understand and use behavior to assess leaders and develop them, yourself and teams to full potential."

John Maxwell, Best Selling Leadership Author and Speaker

"As Base Commander at Lackland AFB, I witnessed the positive impact of the RightPath tools and Jerry Mabe's coaching ability on our senior civilians' leadership development. RightPath's assessments were very helpful in identifying the differences in our staff members and how to use those differences to build a stronger team while developing our team members' leadership skills."

Pat Fogarty, Colonel (Ret.) USAF, Senior Engineer, Joint Staff, Pentagon and previously Base Commander, Lackland AFB

Jerry W. Mabe

CONTENTS

Develop You, Develop Your Team … on the RightPath

CHAPTER 1

CREATING A CULTURE OF DEVELOPMENT

In today's tough economic climate, organizations are looking for ways to be more profitable, more efficient, and more effective. Individuals are looking for ways to secure their position and future opportunities as an integral part of their career success. Together, organizations and leaders must also find the best way to deal with the speed of change, take care of clients, lead the way in the marketplace, and manage resources, including their most valuable resource – their people.

When budgets are tight, organizations must do more with less, which makes having the right people in the right roles even more critical. In today's fast paced world, associates are more attuned to change and thus, effective teamwork, empowerment, and strong leadership are critical factors for success. *Exceptional leaders and effective teams* don't just happen – they are developed intentionally – and led with purpose. It requires a similar effort and intentionality to build and lead teams as it does to build a market position! In my executive coaching practice and Leadership Continuity consulting (The RightPath approach to succession), I see that in the "heat of the battle," many executives lose sight of this fact.

Talent is the key to success. The following concepts are not new in the workplace: a) Developing your own talents, b) Deploying effectively the talents effectively in your organization, and c) Constructing teams that are solid in the foundations of behavioral talents. However, they are now *more* critical as organizations are doing more with less. Developing leaders to know and grow the talent of the teams that they lead propels both individuals and organizations to the next level of success. Come along and we'll show you some tried and tested solutions for how it works.

Our company, RightPath Resources Inc., is a leadership and talent development company, delivering innovative web-based tools for leadership development, selection, and retention. We specialize in solutions for teambuilding and leadership development and we want to share the foundation of these solutions with you. Our online assessment tools are the tools of choice for many Fortune 500 and other dynamic, fast-growing companies, entrepreneurial ventures, family businesses, and not-for profit organizations. We are also their partner of choice as they endeavor to grow and develop leaders and talent for the 21st Century.

Decades of experience and relevant research provide clarity to see the challenges that organizations face in selecting, developing, leading and succeeding talent. RightPath has done extensive work with Fortune 500 and Fortune 1000 clients, high net worth family businesses, NFL and major sporting teams, educational institutions, churches and some of the most progressive not-for-profit organizations in the country and around the world. No matter the size or structure, our clients agree that it is important to select and hire the **right** people with the **right** talents for the **right** positions. You must develop your leaders and your future leaders – your bench. Our clients have seen the benefits when their organizations develop strategies to build strong, effective teams that work smarter, especially in tough economic times. However, the overriding theme we come across again and again is that strong culture and leadership practices unquestionably start at the top in great organizations – but don't remain there.

> **The most excellent of leaders build
> a *Culture of Development* that starts with themselves
> and doesn't end until everyone in the organization
> is given a path to become the best they can be.**

A **Culture of Development** does two incredibly powerful things. First, it allows honesty, transparency and freedom resulting from openly acknowledging that there are *no* perfect leaders. Secondly, it creates a focus on getting better – consistent and committed to the process of developing and improving. This **Culture of Development** involves and affects both the leader and those they lead. It acknowledges that imperfection exists but it doesn't excuse, allow, subsidize, or accept standing still. A **Culture of Development** will not condone talent staying mired in the past or the present – it mandates and drives growth on both a personal and organizational level!

Great leaders who build great organizations have a passion for development and it cascades, not trickles, from the top down not the other way around. RightPath partners with organizations by delivering objective tools – yes, metrics for leadership and talent! Leaders love it when they realize we can accurately measure behavioral talents and have easy access to online assessment suites to measure leadership attributes and whole-life career elements. Developing your people and their talents to be their best moves your company to be its best, hire the best talent and to retain and develop those that are hired – all keys to better performance.

This book is a companion to our online, validated behavioral profiles called RightPath® Path4/6. (See Page 206 for more information on the validation of the tools.) It is our hope that as you walk through the core elements of behavioral talent as measured in these tools, sharing real-life examples, offering stories from great leaders and bookending our commentary with solid research from the industry, you will gain valuable insight into your own talents as well as those you lead. We also aim to help you: a) Better understand those around you and their natural behavioral talents, b) Know how best to build your teams, c) Learn how to effectively mobilize talent within your organization, and d) Retain the talent that you have invested in.

If you are looking to take your own talents to the next level, this book will provide solid solutions. If you are working with people that you can't quite figure out how to facilitate their development, this book holds just the keys you need to unlock the mystery. If you want to know the secrets of building solid, high performing teams, then you've come to the right place. Whether you are a team leader or an individual contributor, discovering your own talents and those of the people you work with will make a positive impact on your day-to-day life as well as your success in the workplace.

First, we'll look briefly at talents and what they entail. Then we will discuss Strengths and Struggles as related to these talents. (Note: Struggles are *not* weaknesses.) We will lead you to an understanding of these elements for yourself as well as for those you lead, work, and interact with. You'll quickly see why understanding "hard-wired" behavior is critical to individual and organizational performance.

"Hard-wired" Behavior is the term used to describe a person's natural behavioral tendencies or "go to" behaviors. These behaviors, we believe, are set in the womb, or may be considered "the hand you were dealt" at birth. Even though a person can exhibit learned behaviors in addition to those that they are naturally hard-wired for, under stress, duress, or deadline, people naturally revert back to their hard-wired, "go to" behaviors.

Path4, our online, four-factor behavioral assessment, will be the foundation on which to discuss how behavioral talents play out in the workplace and relationships. Understanding both sides of the "behavioral coin" will allow you to see yourself and those around you more clearly. We will guide you to analyze how this information relates to teamwork and then move into the critical area of leadership development –your own and the development of those around you.

Next, in order to talk developmentally, we'll introduce you to the deeper insight of our six-factor profile, Path6. Using a medical analogy, Path6 is the MRI to the X-ray we call Path4. Just as an X-ray is a quick diagnostic tool in medicine, Path4 gives a quick behavioral read. Then, Path6 gives a deeper more diagnostic read like an MRI does showing greater detail of the same subject. Path4 and Path6 internally validate each other offering the RightPath tools a competitive advantage when using them together.

Once you understand the key concepts of talents, Strengths, Struggles, and teaming by understanding Path4; our discussion of Path6 will help you see the deeper elements of behavior. We will look at the underlying nuances and motivations beneath those behaviors. Most importantly, you will learn the power of how *predictable* behavior can be. Our clients greatly value these tools and use them to hire, develop teams and grow their leaders. <u>It is not necessary to take the Path4 and Path6 profiles to benefit from the information in this book</u>. Behavioral principles will be explained using real life illustrations to help you understand behavioral factors at work and as you see them in daily life.

Subfactors are another unique element of Path6 and a RightPath competitive difference in the assessment marketplace. The MRI of Path6 is perhaps the most important and powerful tool to use in making smart people-related decisions in your organization. The chapters related to Path6 and its subfactors include a case study example to help you see how they play out in behavior and motivations.

At the end of each chapter we provide a Coach's Notes section for you to record observations about yourself, those you work with, and your team. We encourage you to use this space to mark some self-coaching notes as well as notes to help you coach and develop others while these insights are still fresh from your reading.

CHAPTER 2

EXPLORING TALENT

Talents are "*any* recurring patterns of behavior . . . that can be productively applied *(or that one can learn to apply)*."[1]

With the advent of reality television, there is unprecedented discussion of talent, or lack thereof, in our day-to-day lives. We even pay "texting rates apply" to vote on talent we see on screen. Take command of the remote control and you will find shows about people with talents (and non-talents) who are doing their best to dance, sing, cook, and generally make a spectacle of themselves on national television. Talent, however, is not an invention of the age of reality television. Nor is talent a function of artistic ability or the entertainment industry alone. Rather, talent is an inherent part of every single human being – developed or dormant.

We all – every single one of us – possess talent. In fact, we all possess multiple talents and these talents are deeply rooted in our natural hard-wired behavioral tendencies. We will talk more of talents throughout the book but for now, let's consider some of the research that tells us why this is such an important facet when it comes to leadership and organizational success.

---

[1] FBATR Page 71

7

In investigating the issue of talents in the work place, Buckingham and Coffman discovered something about excellent managers. In their Gallup published book: *First Break All the Rules: What the World's Greatest Managers Do Differently*, the research revealed that excellent managers "select for **talent** … not simply experience, intelligence, or determination." [2] This book remains perhaps the single largest research in American business history, spanning two million employees, eighty thousand managers, and four hundred companies. The authors discovered that hard-wired behavioral talents matter more in exceptional leadership than education or experience. The best way to unlock excellent performance in leaders and individual contributors is to match that individual's talents and his or her role.

The authors of this book contend that people who are deploying their natural behavioral talents are more productive, easier to lead, and experience greater feelings of success. Furthermore, the data in the Gallup research shows that where people's talents are recognized and developed in an organization, profitability increases.[3] My experience in RightPath leads me to wholeheartedly agree with their findings.

Best-selling author and friend of RightPath, John Maxwell, summarized this concept nicely in The 360° Leader.

"Moving someone from a job they hate to the right job can be life changing. One executive I interviewed said he moved a person on his staff to four different places in the organization, trying to find the right fit. Because he'd placed her wrong so many times, he was almost ready to give up on her. But he knew she had great potential, and she was right for the organization. Finally, after he found the right job for her, she was a star!

Trying to get the right person in the right job can take a lot of time and energy. Lets' face it. Isn't it easier for a leader to just put people where it is most convenient and get on with the work? Once again, this is an area where leaders' desire for action can work against them. Don't be afraid to move people around if they're not shining the way you think they could."[4]

---

[2] FBATR Page 67
[3] FBATR Page 37
[4] The Maxwell Daily Reader, Page 14

Throughout this book I will refer to the use of talents – **or productively applied behaviors** – as the means by which to match people and positions. Talents, in my opinion and through the research I have done, cannot be taught. Rather, you must select and develop them. To further support this proposition, consider competency modeling. This approach died in the 1990's because it didn't produce any effective changes in leadership!

In order to select talents you must first be able to recognize and measure them before you attempt to match them to the roles you are trying to fill in your organization. You also must be able to measure the "successful behaviors" that match a specific role. We will discuss how to identify talents and success factors through measuring natural "hard-wired" behavioral tendencies in Chapter 5. First, let's consider the overarching issues of talents – in ourselves, in those around us and in the workplace.

Why don't all people choose to operate in the realm of their natural, behavioral talents?

It seems like a no-brainer to choose a job or career path that suits your talents. But, it is not always so easy. Parental pressure, status and financial reasoning dictate the majority of career choices particularly in American culture. While this tendency may ease up somewhat as the economy continues to struggle, for decades parents have steered their children toward career paths that are socially, financially, and culturally desirable. A college education and graduate degrees have become the norm and yet jobs for these graduates are not guaranteed. The average completion time for a college degree is exceeding six years! The job market, in fact, has taken a hard hit in recent years. While we hope to see recovery soon (I define recovery as when our 201-K's go back to being 401-K's!), it will not happen overnight and the labor force will far outweigh the career openings for some time to come.

I predate Generation X as might many people reading this book. If you are like me, at some point along the line, you've made some important discoveries. Most Baby Boomers have discovered (recently or in the past) that although we were working in jobs that were supposed to earn us a fine living and make us happy, we weren't so happy after all. Job security in a single company and a career in one particular industry – lasting for decade upon decade – are things of the past. That was the job market of our parents and that working reality is all but gone. People under the age of fifty today will expect to have multiple jobs and even multiple careers – not just in their lifetime, but in a single decade. In fact, this is what Generation Y does of its own volition. While Baby Boomers may find themselves feeling restless and wanting to make the best use of our time and energy, the generations after us thrive on restlessness and often define success as including some sense of transience.

Whether caused by a slowed economy, an aging workforce, or the new ideas for Gen X'ers and beyond, the cause is different but the results are much the same – if job seekers and hiring managers are not intentional. Let's consider a couple of examples from both the job seeking and hiring side.

Individuals raised in a time of plenty often enter into the workforce with a focus on financial remuneration and personal flexibility rather than considering the best fit for their talents. I once heard a mother belittle her son's announcement that he wanted to become a high school teacher and coach. She quickly reminded him that he liked nice cars and enjoyed going on luxurious vacations. Whose preferences were those? The words came out of the mother's mouth, projected straight onto the college senior. The young man was on track with consideration of his education, behavioral talents, values, and passions. His mother, on the other hand, assumed that earning potential to match the lavish lifestyle he'd been given as a child and youth were more important than the right talent or passionate 'fit' for him as he chose his career path. Another parent, this time with a daughter in college, encouraged her to pursue a career in the field of finance and accounting. The twenty-three year-old graduating senior, had a passion for photography, but she was baited by the higher salary and more solid job options. Ultimately, she took her parents' advice and got her degree in accounting, disregarding her passion. She found a job right out of college, and signed up to work on her Master's degree part-time. After just months in her first job, she was already restless and began to apply for positions elsewhere. Will this restlessness that causes her to scan the horizon for different opportunities pass or will it mark her career in this industry for years to come? Only time will tell.

Within hiring organizations, this tendency causes challenges too. Imagine the hiring manager who added the young woman right out of college. He has now invested six months in her training and already she is looking around at options elsewhere. He certainly has not yet had time to recoup his company's investment in her. Or, what about the person who hires the "wanna be" coach into a job in sales or administration? Do they have any chance of getting his best out of him if his heart really was on the playing field or on court with kids rather than in corporate America? Would these organizations be better off to hire older, experienced, displaced workers with good "fit" for the job rather than youngsters who may not be rightly motivated in their career pursuits straight out of college?

Such circumstances have great implications for today's up and coming workforce. In some organizations we find people pursuing the career that Mommy or Daddy steered them to by guilt, financial incentive, or perhaps even well-intended advice. We find many organizations full of mid-level managers who have become not only disillusioned with their jobs, but who feel unfulfilled because their talents are not being adequately employed and who struggle to stay fully engaged as time marches on. This is precisely why employee engagement surveys came to life. In an environment where the longevity of a solid paycheck is no longer guaranteed, many people are left wondering if the job they are in is really the best use of their talents and abilities. In many cases, it is not.

We often overlook how this impacts work teams. The mismatches happen in a host of ways. Employees seek and accept the wrong jobs. Hiring managers choose the wrong people for a particular role or team. People on both the hiring, selection, and job seeking side are often not sure of exactly what they are looking for. Executives and managers may believe an individual with a good work ethic or a solid education should be able to do any job they are given. While this may be true much of the time, performance levels are not always optimal if the fit isn't right. In the competitive environment and downsizing of today, people *need* to be high performers in their roles for a company in order to truly succeed. Also, consider how long someone is able to perform well when they are constantly swimming upstream or "going against the grain".

Many years ago, corporations could get away with treating people like a "captive" workforce. They could hire them, issue them paychecks and expect them to not only operate effectively but to be grateful for the job they held. Issuing orders was all that was needed to have people trained. Workers, once trained, were expected to fulfill their roles in a motivated and responsive manner. Gratitude, training, and an employee's sense of obligation are not sure-fire guarantees of success – nor do they guarantee longevity in a job today. In the twenty-first century, people of all ages want to employ their talents and engage in efforts that they are passionate about – meaningful work.

Whether a young individual new to the workforce or a discouraged, seasoned member of the workforce who is looking to make a change, employees seem to care more and more about passion, significance, and job fit. If an individual does settle for a job that will simply provide a paycheck and "fill the gap," he or she cannot be counted on to stay in that role long-term. Most individuals will jump at a better "fit" when it comes along and are likely to continue actively looking for that "better" fit opportunity. These restless individuals are "high flight risk" for the organizations in which they work.

How do we motivate ourselves?

How do we motivate those who work for us?

What does it mean to hire smarter?

The solution is this: we come to understand, appreciate,

engage and further develop the behavioral talents that

our people *already naturally* possess.

As I said earlier, every person possesses natural, behavioral talents. These are the behaviors that come easily to a person and which affect the way they operate day-to-day in all areas of life – including work. Some people have a natural sense of consensus. Some individuals have a knack for details. Some are collaborative and others creative. Some are decisive and some are good at assessing risk. The description of people's individual composition of talents is broad and varied, yet these talents can be accurately assessed and measured.

The Workplace Is Not Merely a Collection of Individuals – Rather It is a Collection of Individual Talents.

Why does this matter? As discussed, matching "good people" to jobs is not the most successful method for filling roles – although the majority of hiring managers try to do just that. Most of us can think of an occasion where a diligent, nice, and hardworking person failed in a job that simply didn't match his or her talents. And so, matching behavioral talents of the person to roles is much more effective and productive for the organization *and* much more fulfilling for the individual.

To Succeed in the Marketplace for Both Employee and Employer – Talents Must Be Aligned on Both a Personal and Organizational Level.

Successful companies value the talent they possess but they don't stop there. They also develop and invest in the talents of their people at all levels of the organization. People doing what they like to do, what they are naturally hard-wired to do well and what they believe in produces a win-win situation for employees and the organization. The employee is happy, productivity increases, profits go up, and turnover decreases. The employer gains increased productivity and a stable workforce.

So then, how do you identify behavioral talent *and* match it to the positions in your organization? Furthermore, how do you develop it to its fullest potential in your organization? How do you then protect your investment and retain that talent for the long haul? Writer Peter Capelli, as he writes for the Harvard Business Review, says:

"One thing is for sure: as the early years of the new century unfold, executives will be challenged to abandon their old ways of thinking and adopt more creative ways of managing, retaining, and, yes, releasing their talent. Those who begin this difficult process now will be one step ahead of the game.[5]

Talent is the most important corporate resource especially in challenging times. And understanding talent is the key to putting the right people in the right roles and building successful teams and organizations.

It is Hard to Take the Wrong Talent Match and Try to Make It Right.

Ask anybody who has worked in a job where they lacked the natural talents that would lend them success and they will tell you it is exhausting work. Many of us can relate to this in "summer job" experiences! A very reserved person will eventually be worn out and depleted if placed in a role that requires a large volume of face-to-face

---

[5] A Market-Driven Approach to Retaining Talent, Peter Capelli, Harvard Business Review, January—February 2000

interaction with people. A spontaneous person may find sitting at a desk all day to be torturous. Someone with a high attention to detail and great ability to focus may become quickly frustrated in a very fluid environment. In any of these cases, it would be difficult for the individual to thrive in the mis-matched position. Individuals are better off in roles where their natural talents are put to good use not where they have to constantly adapt and stretch their natural behavioral preferences.

People perform at their best when they are in roles that go in the direction of their natural talents. This fit allows them to "swim downstream with the current" of their talents rather than to "swim upstream" against it. Work is more enjoyable and efficient when you are aligned with your natural talents. Think about a time when your work seemed more joyful than burdensome, when you easily lost track of time in the flow of what you were working on. Most likely, the tasks at hand and behavioral talents they required were a good fit for you in that season.

Next, think of a time when your days at work seemed to drag on forever. Consider the projects that you came to dislike or even despise. Was the work at hand suited to your natural talents or were you being asked to operate out of your comfort zone? Did you have a need for control in that season but found you had none? Were the tasks at hand and interactions of the day draining rather than energizing for you? It takes a great deal of energy to operate outside of your natural behavioral talents, progress is slow and success often elusive. Mis-matched talents and tasks not only slows or impairs effectiveness, they also wear out your most important resource – your people. Productivity at work, and employee satisfaction and engagement are highest when people's behavioral talents are matched to the positions they are fulfilling.

The foundational key to employee engagement is matching the talents of the person to the success factors of the job.

15

Talents and the Search for Significance

A person's career path is rarely a straight line. I certainly have some stories to tell from my own life, both positive and negative about individual contributors and leaders in their search for significance. If you think for a few moments, I bet you can recall a story or two of a job taken or career decision that you or someone close to you made which turned out for the worse instead of the better. Sometimes we fall into the trap of chasing a dream that belongs to someone other than ourselves. Other times we choose a path that is not in line with our natural talents. Or, we may take a job simply out of necessity rather than excitement. The good news is that discovering your natural talents involves the lessons learned in those sorts of detours. Knowing what you *don't* want and the things you do not naturally excel in allows you to make better choices moving forward in the search for fulfillment and significance. From deploying natural talents we move to a deeper need of the "Call" on our lives to do what we were created to do. Os Guinness, apologist and philosopher points out the dangers of ignoring the path of growth and the "Call":

"Crises created by a contradiction between successful careers and satisfying work are even more fateful. For when we set out in youth and choose careers for external reasons – such as lure of the salary, the prestige of position, or pressure from parents and peers – we are setting ourselves up for frustration later in life if the work does not equally suit us for internal reasons, namely our giftedness and calling. 'Success' may then flatter us on the outside as "significance" eludes us from the inside."[6]

Individuals who follow their talents and passions are both inspired and inspirational. They are the stuff movies and books are made of. The actual work an inspired person is doing may or may not be of great significance in the grand scheme of things but as individuals, they are often the impact-makers of this world. By connecting their talents and passions, they plug into a positive energy that moves them forward

---

[6] *The Call*, by Os Guinness, pp. 150-151, © 1998 Word Publishing, Nashville, TN.

on the road to personal significance and fulfillment. These people have the potential to become the greatest leaders and highest performers of our time. They have discovered the key of identifying talents and unfolding them in their own lives, and that helps them produce good outcomes for everyone. Such leaders are now in a position to help develop others to do the same, resulting in the achievement of greater success at work, at home and in our communities.

Coach's Notes:

Finding what we are created ("wired") to do, brings us closer to satisfaction and significance. And, as we find satisfaction and significance, we are better able to lead and guide others to do the same. Record your initial thoughts on some of the things you were created ("wired") to do.

CHAPTER 3

STRENGTHS, STRUGGLES,
AND WHAT ABOUT WEAKNESSESS?

So far we have talked quite a bit about talent. If your own personal set of talents is the car that you drive, then the Strengths and Struggles resulting from those talents are the gas pedal and brake. Strengths that stem from our behavioral talents are usually pretty easy to identify, particularly when a behavioral tendency in a person is very strong. These are our wired or natural "go to" traits. Strengths, like the gas pedal, help to propel us into positive motion. Struggles (things that we are not naturally adept at), like a brake, halt or impede our progress and success. Working constantly within struggles creates drag or friction like the brake. It causes fatigue.

What many people don't realize, is that pure 'non-talents' are not usually the greatest struggles which hinder a person's success.

**Rather, Strengths over-done are more often
the greatest hindrance
to a person's success.**

And so, self-awareness related to your own Strengths and Struggles allows you to be more objective in understanding yourself and those around you.

To that point, having now coached a significant number of Fortune 500 and Fortune 1000 executives as well as high net worth individuals, I have been asked the difference in coaching these levels of high tier leaders versus working with mid-level leaders. The answer has become clear over time. Higher-level executives' Struggles are much more likely to be their "go to" Strengths *over-done*. This 'two sided' coin concept of a Strength over-done becoming a struggle is very real and frequently seen in the executive level. The reason for this frequency is that overdoing a "go to" Strength makes for an easy blind spot. Often these Strengths are the very things that propelled the executive to his or her current level. Over-doing that success factor becomes an insidious blind spot without incredible self-awareness, assessment, and objective feedback like coaching. And every high level executive knows, the higher you climb the harder it becomes to get honest, objective feedback – it has become commonplace for me to see a high level executive take our LQ360 (multi-rater leadership assessment) and then use **none** of their lowest scoring items addressed in the first draft they make of their leadership development plan (LDP)! Self-awareness, assessment, and objective feedback are the cure.

Strength defined: *A Strength is a person's best or "strongest" talent, behaviorally speaking.* Strengths are usually behaviors that a person feels compelled to use in their daily life at work, home and play. For some it may be an attention to detail, for others it may be the ability to work collaboratively, or it may be the ability to act decisively. The list of talents is endless. However, the key to success is to utilize your talents as much as possible and minimize required use in areas in which you are not so talented. If you aren't sure what your talents are, just ask those around you what they notice that you are naturally adept at – and you'll soon see that they can readily identify some of your most obvious talents.

If you were playing golf and discovered that you had a talent for putting, your handicap might improve significantly. Deciding to lean too hard on this particular talent, however, might lead you to want to play the whole game with your putter – and then you'd have a problem. You can't play an entire game of golf effectively with a putter. Even the golfer with the best putting game on the golf course needs to know when to use a different club. In fact, a great golfer uses a wide variety of the golf clubs he carries.

Every Strength Has a Corresponding Struggle. We refer to this as the "two-sided coin" of behaviors. Typically, the talents and abilities that lead to one's success, when over-done, become one's greatest challenge or Struggle. For example: If a person is able to work with high attention to detail for long periods of time, this talent might be the core of his or her success as a neurosurgeon, a financial analyst, or a computer programmer. These Strengths are a perfect fit for roles requiring high attention to detail and focus.

There are also Struggles, however, that correlate to this trait as well. Someone who is meticulous in their work may at times become too picky. A person who is always highly prepared may rely too heavily on that preparedness and become inflexible when trying to solve a problem or meet a deadline. A person who is structured and organized may display Strengths and Struggles listed below. Look for the "over-done" correlation between the two lists.

Strengths	Struggles
- establishes systems	- may over-rely on procedures and rules
- organized and scheduled	- tends to be inflexible
- accurate with details	- may focus on details and miss the goal

Struggles are a natural progression or byproduct of Strengths or as highlighted earlier, Struggles are often your best Strengths over-done. In fact, the correlation between Strengths and their resulting or corresponding Struggles is what allows us to better predict behavior and view it more objectively. Understanding the balance between Strengths and Struggles allows leaders and team members to have more realistic expectations about human behavior as well as its predictability.

Struggles in the Workplace

Great managers focus on an individual's Strengths, and expect and deal with the corresponding Struggles as much as they can. Although our American culture tends to tout improving weaknesses, emphasizing Strengths is the more common theme among great managers according to the Gallup survey cited earlier. Why emphasize Strengths rather than focus on improving Struggles? Because behavior is hard to change, especially behaviors that accompany our best talents. It is costly and difficult to change human behavior. Working with the flow of one's natural talents is much easier than going against the grain of those talents over time. Effort needs to be made however to help team members not only embrace their talents but also recognize the resulting Struggles that stem from those talents. **RightPath disagrees with overlooking your Struggles. This has become a too convenient excuse for leaders, especially senior leaders, to not continue their leadership development.** You don't want to change the underlying behavior completely, just temper it in its most extreme manifestations – i.e. where the Strength becomes a Struggle.

We believe assessments that overly focus a leader on his or her Strengths tend to be a great marketing ploy that leads to inflated egos. Such tools lead to a sense that "I'm great! Now let's see where you are great!" This approach can dangerously reinforce the "over-done" parts of Strengths which become Struggles. In coaching, I have come behind such assessments and had to then coach leaders to deal with the blind spots that these strengths-focused assessments can reinforce.

Non-Talents

It is normal to think first of non-talents when we use the word Struggles. When someone asks you what your struggles are, typically things that you do not do well come to mind. These deficiencies are not necessarily your greatest weaknesses however. In most cases they are things that do not come naturally for you. Non-talents are abilities that are likely never going to be easy for you, and they are very difficult for you to develop on your own. While you may gain some ground in them, they are never going to become your Strengths. For example, one of my team members is not a particularly precise person. She can work on skills like proof reading, slowing down and focusing more on details but those skills will never be the strongest tools in her toolbox. On the flip side however, she is naturally a great multi-tasker. She is a flexible and intuitive generalist which makes her a valuable part of our team. Has she learned to help compensate for her non-talent in precision? Yes, she makes lists and double checks things using systems to force herself to slow down. Will precision ever become a talent for her? Not likely. Her natural wiring is to move quickly and flexibly so she will always prefer to lean that way if given the chance.

While it is possible for her to become more detailed, more focused, and have a higher attention to accuracy, doing so takes work and a great deal of energy. She would not want to have those task requirements become the most important elements of her job because if her job depended largely on her overcoming those struggles, she would quickly become frustrated. She can, and has, learned to be aware of this Struggle in life and work and she has put in measures to help compensate for it. For instance, she makes lists. She also doesn't turn in work as soon as it is finished, but instead she allows enough time to reread it once more before submission. If her job required a high attention to detail all day, every day, she would need more than just those compensations to perform at a high level. However, it would come at a high price for her energy-wise, frustration-wise, and with regard to her personal sense of fulfillment.

When I talk about managing your Struggles, the word I prefer to use is "overcome." The goal is not ever to expect to turn your Struggles into your Strengths, but rather to diffuse their potential for causing problems by overcoming them. The first critical step is to be fully aware of them. Then, *overcoming* struggles means neutralizing their negative impact by moving them towards having a positive impact in your work or relationships. They likely will never become your Strengths but once neutralized, or overcome, they are no longer such a hindrance.

Some Struggles such as spontaneity or disorganization are more easily overcome than others. Often goals are the catalyst necessary to get the process of overcoming underway. For instance, let's look at a very busy, not-so-structured person who has a goal of achieving a Master's degree while working full-time. That person may quickly find that the goal of obtaining that degree is just what they needed to lead them to make an effort to become more organized and structured – to overcoming their natural spontaneity. The drive to the goal makes the effort to neutralize the Struggles worthwhile.

In this instance, an individual is adding a new "Learned Behavior" capacity as a layer on top of their natural or "Hard-Wired Behavior." Although they may become very good at executing their new behavioral pattern, they will still tend to revert to their natural, underlying behavioral tendency under pressure or stress. But, where time and circumstances allow and particularly where goals drive, individuals can overcome Struggles that are negatively impacting their work or relationships.

When Strengths Are Overdone They Become Struggles.

There really are two kinds of Struggles. One is the Struggle which we just described – it stems from an area of non-talent. The fact that our assessment tool measures extended behavioral talents on a two-sided continuum says it all. No single person does everything well. And, there are Strengths on each side of the behavioral continuum for every factor; Strengths of the person who is Directing *or* Accommodating, of the one who is Engaging *or* the one who is Reserved, and so on.

Furthermore, most people are aware of the things they do not do well, naturally. I don't deal well with a long conversation to get to a point. I do not have great patience. I tend to be initially skeptical rather than giving others the benefit of the doubt. These are some of the areas that I personally work on to overcome.

The second type of Struggle is not non-talent but rather it stems from our greatest areas of talent – our Strengths. When strengths are over-done or over-relied-upon they become Struggles. This flavor of Struggle is often the one that others see more readily in each of us. Had I not told you I was naturally skeptical, you may never have known this fact. But, the Struggles related to my Strengths over-done - like my impatience - are harder to hide.

It is natural to rely on your Strengths especially when they help pave the way to success. It is easy to rely on these Strengths too much and to the detriment of our success. Why is this occurrence common? People naturally gravitate towards their Strengths and when the pressure is on, they tend to lean even more heavily into them. That's why we call them "go to" behaviors.

Strengths over-done may be a new concept to you but I bet you can now identify them more easily. Follow along with me for a moment. Have you ever encountered a decisive, confident, quick-minded, person who has been "right" so often that he or she now seems unable to hear ideas from anybody else? Or, think of the compassionate, patient, supportive people who help everyone out until one day their inability to say "no" makes their Struggle apparent –they have worn themselves out. Or maybe, you have met the methodical person with great attention to detail who struggle with "paralysis by analysis."

Of the two types of struggles – **non-talents and strengths over-done** – the second is harder for individuals to recognize because the intensity that leads from Strength to Struggle usually occurs a little at a time, over time. Often individuals are unaware of the point at which the behavior that typically brings them success starts to cause troubles (blind spots) instead. If the shift is perpetuated under stress it is not likely to be noticed immediately either. The key, however, is recognizing both types of Struggles and doing what you can to neutralize the effect of non-talents and tone down Strengths over-done for a reversal into a more positive range. This information all points to the reason for and the power of accurate and objective assessment.

Struggles (Rather Than Strengths) Are the Key to Relationships

Recognizing and employing our strengths is critical to successful *Results* at work and at home. Understanding Struggles – our own and others' – is key to successful *Relationships* at work and at home.

For instance, let's consider a highly engaging extrovert who likes to have fun all the time. His easy rapport and outgoing nature make him easy for clients to talk to. He's persistent and he likes the people-related aspects of his job. Although he fits his role, it can also be said that sometimes he is talkative, overly optimistic, has a high need for attention and often doesn't finish what he starts. Let's call this extrovert, Joe.

Joe's highly verbal nature and high energy irritate Susan because the "noise" causes a distraction when she is trying to work. Susan is more reserved and enjoys a quiet, focused work environment that is free from unnecessary distractions. Although she knows Joe is good at his job, the traits that make him successful in it can quickly exasperate and exhaust her when they're unleashed in the office – especially since the Strengths he exhibits are polar opposite to her own.

Susan is reserved, quiet and serious. These traits translate to Strengths in her role of managing processes in the company. But, these same traits can also make her seem cold and distant to Joe who loves to collaborate and tries desperately to engage her in conversation. In fact, when she does engage she usually has something pessimistic rather than positive to say. He wonders why she's always so withdrawn when he's

26

"just trying to be friendly." Like Joe, she is a top performer in her job.

Joe and Susan are polar opposites. In the example I just gave, they don't seem to like each other much but it doesn't have to be that way. You see, if rather than begrudging each other their Struggles (resulting from Strengths overdone), they would embrace their complementary Strengths; they'd be better able to meet in the middle. Susan would realize that Joe likes to feel connected to the people he works with, so she would make the effort to engage in brief conversations with him more often. Joe would realize that Susan needs time to process information before discussing it, so he wouldn't expect her to brainstorm on the spot. Instead he might share information, making sure he's not interrupting her workflow, and circle back around to her once she's had time to think about that information.

Neither Joe nor Susan is right or better than the other. They are just different. In fact, they are polar opposites. The key is for them both to recognize these "opposite behaviors," be open about them, communicate well, and give grace to one another. Susan will need to say, "Joe, I'm in the middle of a project. Give me half an hour and I will come to catch up with you." Joe will need to preface his discussion with, "Susan, I need ten minutes when you get time. Really, just ten! (And stick to his word.) Let me know when a good time is for you." As they learn to accept and appreciate their differences, they will find it easier to meet in the middle between their polar opposite Strengths. In the process they will become better teammates and perform better in their respective jobs. As the process of understanding each other takes place, both parties will find it easier to address their struggles for the greater good of their relationship and the business. In RightPath Mastering Creative Conflict curriculum, I teach that it is a law of physics that nothing can be sharpened without some friction. They can actually, over time, make each other better leaders.

Strengths are critical for succeeding at work. Struggles are the focus for improving relationships. Anticipating and understanding

Struggles takes practice, but it is worth the effort. Struggles are a source of friction in leadership, teamwork and all relationships but they don't have to be if they are recognized, and accepted with the goal to "overcome" – as much as possible.

In Chapter 23 on Leadership Development, you will have a chance to explore your own Strengths and Struggles in greater detail.

Coach's Notes:

What Strengths are you over-doing that have become a Struggle? Evaluate whether it may be a blind spot for your leadership.

CHAPTER 4

SELF-AWARENESS AND OBJECTIVITY

Self-awareness is the hallmark of great managers and leaders. To me, it is the foundational cornerstone to sustainable leadership development. But, to see yourself as you really are, you must have objectivity. Objectivity starts with an accurate view of yourself and from that point you can then begin to see others much more clearly as well.

To process information accurately and make good decisions demands objectivity. Influential leaders of today share an objectivity that allows them to remove personal bias from assimilation of information and decision-making. Credibility often hinges on a leader's ability to operate in the realm of objectivity.

Being Objective Does Not Come Naturally

What does it mean to be objective? Many correlate the word to being tough-minded or non-emotional or even detached. Some think it is the opposite to the warm, fuzzy side of leadership and relationships. And others might tell you that objectivity means dealing with reality and the truth no matter how challenging it is. A logical person might say that objectivity requires accurate information and leads to logical decisions and good results.

While accurate information is critical to the process, the

29

descriptions above do not reflect true objectivity. Tough mindedness or removing emotion from situations does not make a person objective. In a way, it introduces its own form of bias. Seeing and understanding both sides of the behavioral coin – Strengths and Struggles – are what allow a person to be objective in their view of themselves and others. It truly is the opposite of subjective.

Every single one of us processes information through a skewed filter. Our brains process information, but rarely we ever receive completely accurate information and data for decision-making. Furthermore, the data we do receive is skewed by the filters of our experiences (good or bad), our knowledge base, our environment, and our intellect. That is to say, the lens through which any person sees the world is distorted by "self" and the experiences of self – subjectively, subjective to myself and my experience.

Experience Impacts Objectivity

Past experiences cause us to filter current data. If information received in a situation triggers memories from a past experience, our ability to deal with the current situation objectively, without bias, is limited. Past experience can cause us to jump to conclusions, positive or negative, and affect our decision-making ability.

When interviewing a candidate for a job, a manager might be reminded of a former employee who the candidate resembles. If that former employee was a high performer, the manager might assume the candidate will be also. The converse is also true. Although you'd hope that physical characteristics, personal mannerisms, and such wouldn't affect the way the manager receives and interviews this candidate, instinctively, those factors come into play. However, with formatted interview questions based on an accurate assessment tool in hand, a second round of interviewers and other selection practices in place, objectivity is applied back into a process that otherwise might have been skewed to some degree by a filter of past experience.

That is a simple work related example. Consider also this

additional illustration to see how strong the filter of past experience can be. If you are younger than I am, it is most likely your parents were not alive or were very young children during the Great Depression of the last century. Yet people today can still hold onto a mentality tied back to that time in history. For instance, a friend of mine's parents stack canned goods floor to ceiling in their home. When they come to visit her, they bring coolers and boxes of food, in volume. They were taught by experience and by their parents to conserve and store goods in case they ever need them. Although my friend's pantry and fridge always have more than enough food for her family and her visiting parents as well, they still come with food galore. "Hoarders" are another example of this filter of past experience. They can never comfortably throw away unused articles. Their viewpoint is so engrained that no manner of logic or discussion seems to be able to change the way they operate.

Filters exist in people's minds related to gender, social status, race, and generational differences too. Take such filters a step further and they can become a stereotype or even prejudice. Sometimes such filters (or their more destructive counterpart) come from personal experiences in our past. Other times they are derived from information fed into our experience second hand by parents, friends or the media.

Regardless of the source, experiential filters affect our objectivity and thus we need to learn to recognize those filters. We must reexamine data we receive with those filters turned down or better yet turned off, or replaced where possible. Great leaders are even open to others helping them to "reframe" data if filters are too ingrained. The key to adjusting these filters is self-awareness.

Before Self-Awareness Comes View of Self

Ego – it is a word that conjures up images quickly in the mind. We think perhaps of an egotistical, larger than life character we know in real life or watch on television. The truth is we all have ego and it distorts the way we receive and perceive ourselves and others.

People tend to distort their view of self and others one of two ways. Person A in the model that follows tends to have a higher opinion of self and a more critical view of others. Person B tends to have a more kind view of others and critical view of self. In either case, there's a bias that distorts objectivity. In reality, every person is a blend of Strengths and Struggles and when seen objectively there isn't a skew towards one side or the other. Notice the blind spots are minimized in Person C. This is the key thing that effective coaching does in development – minimizes blind spots.

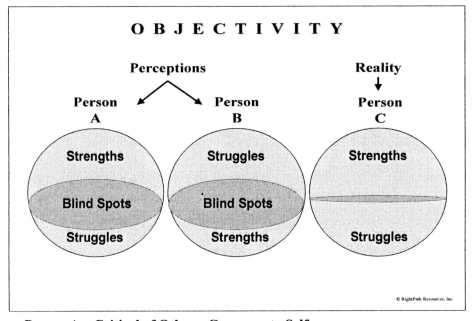

Person A – Critical of Others, Generous to Self

Ego is likely the cause of Person A's bias toward being overly generous in self-evaluation in the diagram above. This person can usually rattle off a list a mile long of what is wrong with their manager, spouse, or kids, but the list of their own Struggles is very short. Many a person who leans this way might even say they didn't have any Struggles at all. And, if you were to ask him or her to write out a list of Strengths for one of those people they are in relationship with, the list would be very small because they tend to focus on the Struggles of others – not their Strengths.

Often, a person who tends to overestimate self will have a corresponding tendency to underestimate others, especially if that person's set of talents is different from their own.

Person B – Critical of Self, Generous to Others

Some readers will have identified with Person A described above, and others are more like Person B. Person B holds himself or herself to a standard of perfection but when it comes to others, this person gives them the benefit of the doubt. Or, if not perfection, this person may just underestimate himself or herself. In doing so, it is likely that Person B is overestimating others. In a mild situation, Person B might just assume another person is better suited to the job. Or taken to the extreme, Person B might assume they may fall short where others would succeed. Fears of taking reasonable risks and competency may affect this person.

The Real World – Everyone Has Strengths, Struggles and Blind Spots

In the diagram, Person C exhibits a balanced approach from which an individual can accurately assess their own Strengths and Struggles. This is also the perspective from which blind spots are minimized and where one can work on developing a balanced perspective. No one is Struggle free. No one is without Strengths either. This is what a "whole person" concept is about.

Relationships are more productive when the individuals in them see both Strengths and Struggles. Being able to anticipate both the strengths and struggles of those you work with and share life with makes things a whole lot easier. This awareness allows us to encourage each other in our Strengths. It also allows us to anticipate Struggles and more importantly, not react or take actions personally thereby allowing us to work together to minimize the impact.

Blind Spots Are Inevitable But Do Not Need To Be Permanent. Helping people see their blind spots can be challenging because human nature leads us to want to believe the best about ourselves. Blindness to

33

Struggles is not usually a result of deliberate choice. Rather, individuals operate in the realm of their experience and circumstances and may be completely oblivious to the blind spots in their behavior. Pointing out a blind spot to a friend may result in a response of denial or defensiveness. In such cases, walking through an example of that behavior may help the blinded person to see.

Sometimes, individuals realize that something is not right but they cannot yet see their blind spot. For instance, a manager might realize that a particular staff member begins avoiding her and doesn't act as nice to her as usual when the month-end draws near. The manager may assume that the staff member is being nice to other people but not her when in fact, it might be the manager's controlling behavior and hyper focus on deadlines (as the month-end nears) that is causing the problem. The staff member, working hard to meet the manager's high expectations, is also trying to deliver results under her increasingly controlling behavior. When this scenario is replayed for the manager, the manager may simply think she is taking charge, being responsible and helping to hold her staff accountable. That viewpoint may be true for the first two weeks of every month, but as the deadlines draw nearer, her need for control and pressure on staff increases to the point where this one staff member has begun to avoid this particular manager during that time frame.

In this example, the manager's behavior is effective much of the time. Staff see her as competent, a good leader, focused and detailed. But when the pressure of deadlines looms closer, effective behaviors go into overdrive and she can shift from being in control of the situation to become controlling over people. Once this blind spot is made evident to the manager, she can modify her behavior in those more pressured times and adjust accordingly.

In addition to our blind spots, behaviorally, which are the things we don't see about ourselves; there are motivations behind our behaviors. These are areas to which *others* are blinded and cannot clearly see. For example, outsiders cannot accurately see your intentions but they can see your actions. And when they do, they often make corresponding judgments concerning the motivation behind those actions. Human nature leads us to tend to consider the effect of circumstances on ourselves, but we often underplay circumstantial issues when assessing the motivations of others. And, we are inclined to justify our own behaviors rather than to give the benefit of the doubt to others.

For instance, if I miss my flight I rationalize that my alarm clock didn't go off on time, traffic was terrible, the elevator was full, and long security lines made being on time impossible. If the person I am due to meet with this afternoon misses his flight, however, he must have been shortsighted and did not give himself enough leeway to make the flight on time.

Although we always have information and usually more accurate information when making judgment calls on ourselves, this is not the case when dealing with others. Psychologists call this "fundamental attribution." That lack of information can cause relational and leadership problems. It is important to do all that we can to understand the individuals we work with day in and day out. We need to recognize not just their behaviors, but also evaluate their behaviors in light of how they are similar or different to our own. We also need to consider the circumstances they are operating within. If we don't, we run the risk of setting up our relationships on the basis of unrealistic expectations and being set up for disappointment, disenchantment and results which do not measure up. Furthermore, this creates a fertile opportunity in which unhealthy conflict can arise.

On the flipside, if personal awareness rules and our expectations are more realistic rather than unrealistic; it is much easier to extend patience, offer encouragement and operate with grace and forgiveness. If our reactions and attitudes towards another person illicit a reciprocal response then grace breeds kindness where harsh words brew conflict.

What does this all mean? Seeing your own blind spots will improve your relationships. If you cannot identify them yet, ask trusted peers and mentors around you what sort of counter-productive behaviors they see in you. Ask them to help you see and know that from this courageous place comes positive change. Additionally, use accurate assessments to help you gain personal objectivity and predict blind spots.

Then, when looking at others use the same frame of reference you'd give to yourself. Look at others through the lens of grace. Give them the benefit of the doubt. Consider if they are like you or different than you. Ask questions to help you understand not just the behavior you see but the motivation and circumstances surrounding that behavior – without the previous inherent assumptions.

Understanding others' behavior sounds complicated, but it doesn't have to be. With an assessment tool to help you objectively measure behavioral traits it becomes easy. Such measurement and an understanding of human behavioral tendencies – those like yours and those different than yours – will revolutionize your leadership and your life. Most executives and leaders I coach are amazed at how quickly and easily they can learn to see and understand behavior with an assessment tool. I've seen it have a life changing impact on leaders. Read on and we will show you how to understand behavior in yourself and others and how to lead effectively based on this information.

Coach's Notes:

Which are you most like — Person A or Person B or Person C (Pg. 32)?

List some of your perceived or potential blind spots below.
(If you aren't sure, ask someone you trust to help identify them.)

CHAPTER 5

MEASURING NATURAL, "HARD-WIRED" BEHAVIOR

Just as each individual has a unique finger print, each individual is also behaviorally unique. While that might seem daunting to think that you have to learn about every single person, there is some good news. Although our exact behavioral makeup is unique to each of us, behaviors are measurable and predictable. A good portion of hardwired behavior is also easily observed – especially once you learn about behavioral factors.

Consider the people you know. Are some of them talkative? Are others logical and serious? Do you know which friends or colleagues would welcome a challenge and which ones would dread the unknown without significant information and forewarning? See! You already can identify some of the behavioral tendencies of the people around you. Let's talk about how to better identify and quantify these behaviors and their resulting Strengths (talents) and Struggles.

Understanding behavior is critical to success in relationships in general; it's especially significant for leaders in the workplace. At work, matching talents (recurring patterns of behavior that are, or can be, productively applied) to roles increases productivity, reduces stress, provides for good health, improves performance, and increases the likelihood of job satisfaction. Accordingly, it's good to know what behaviors will make a person successful in a role or on a team and then select with that fit in mind.

We also need to know clearly what behavioral Struggles we can expect from those we work with. As discussed in the prior chapter, it's essential to be aware of a person's Struggles (non-talents). But, the most important piece of the struggle puzzle is to discover the root cause. Is the Struggle a result of Strengths overdone? Remember that's where the Strength when taken to the extreme becomes unproductive and "takes over." Or, is the root cause of a Struggle due to due non-talents? This truth results from the fact that most people are aware of the behaviors they are not naturally adept at.

But, most people are not aware of the blind spots that result from their Strengths being over-done. Under pressure or stress individuals naturally tend to gravitate to their strongest behavioral traits and thus run the risk of pushing into the unproductive side of these behaviors.

How Do We Measure Behavior And Identify Strengths and Struggles?

The science behind measuring hard-wired, natural behavioral traits (a form of psychometrics) is just that, science. Behavior can be measured in a realistic, statistical, objective manner even to the point where behavior can be predicted based on such information. This objective measurement and predictive application is the most valuable tool for individuals and organizations trying to make the most of themselves and the people they work with.

*These behavioral concepts hold the key
to high performing individuals, teams and leaders
within organizations. Most importantly, understanding these
concepts gives you the keys to developing yourself and others.*

Just as I can measure someone's height, weight and body mass index, I also can measure their behavioral attributes. Behavioral tendencies fall along a bell curve where the extremes are less common and the mean (i.e. midpoint in a standard distribution) is more common. To simplify this concept, consider the average height of a full-grown man. A man's height might range from say three feet to eight feet. Most of the population, however, will fall between five and six feet tall. There are extremely short men in the world and extremely tall men but the majority of the adult, male population will land towards the middle ground of five-foot-and-some-inches in height. As an example, the mid-point (mean) in the United States is five-feet and nine-and-a-half inches tall.

Continuing with the height analogy, consider that a very short individual may wear platform shoes, walk on stilts or employ the use of a ladder in order to change a light bulb in a ceiling fixture located seven feet above his head. The same task, though, would require no adaptation or physical props for a man who is nearly eight feet tall. The tall man would be able to simply reach up, unassisted, and swap the bulb. If you needed to hire a person for a job that required changing 1000 light bulbs a day, situated in fixtures mounted on a ten-foot-high ceiling, it would be faster and easier for the tall man to meet the demands of the job than the shorter man. Conversely, changing lights on a pathway or in the tighter space, the shorter man gains the faster, easier edge. Taller or shorter is not right or wrong – just different.

Behavioral talents may not be as readily identifiable as height, but, they are indeed observable and measurable. How they are measured may surprise you. An individual's educational credentials, work

39

experience or personal interests may or may not be correlated to what his or her behavioral talents are. And so, we need a way to objectively measure behavior and then look at it on a continuum of possibilities. This sort of measurement provides the information needed to understand individuals and furthermore to develop, coach, lead, and mentor them. It is needed for building and leading strong, diverse teams as well as to help efficient teams be more effective.

RightPath Path4 and Path6 behavioral profiles offer this accurate measurement. They are the online, validated behavioral assessments of choice for successful organizations across the country and around the globe including Fortune 500 and Fortune 1000's, NFL Executive Teams, family businesses, and successful Not-for-Profits.

An Overview of RightPath® Path4 (the X-Ray)

Path4 measures four behavioral factors on a two-sided continuum to display a total of eight distinct behavioral traits. There are Strengths and Struggles associated with all eight behavioral traits. Scores in the factors are distributed in a bell curve so that the population is divided into left-side, mid-range and right-side scoring areas. Traits listed on either side of the continuum are opposite to one another.

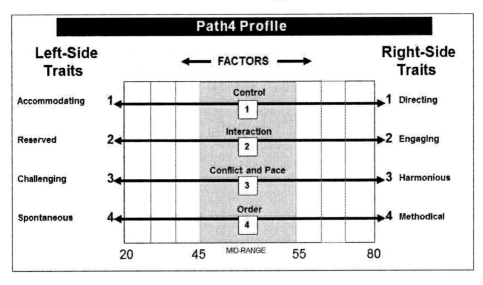

For each of the traits measured in Path4, one third of the general population scores on average to the left-side of the continuum (scores of 44 or lower). One third of the general population scores in the clustered mid-range section of the graph marked as scores from 45 to 55. And, one third of the general population falls to the right-side where scores are reported from 56 to 80. This means that for whichever section you fall in on the graph, two thirds of the population is different than you and one third is like you in that trait. If you fall on the right-side or left-side, one third of the general population is like you, one-third is different than you, and one-third is your *polar opposite*. Does that impact how we develop and work? It had better!

BEHAVIORAL CONTINUUM

1/3	1/3	1/3
1 Accommodating	Mid-Range	Directing 1
2 Reserved	Mid-Range	Engaging 2
3 Challenging	Mid-Range	Harmonious 3
4 Spontaneous	Mid-Range	Methodical 4

1/3 of the general population scores in each region.

Standardized scores for each of the four factors are displayed on a horizontal continuum with left-side, right-side, and mid-range scoring regions. Approximately one third of the population scores in each region.

The image above helps us to see the traits and the segments, behaviorally, for each 1/3 of the population. Individuals in the mid-range section whose scores are 45 to 55 will exhibit behaviors from both sides of the continuum. For instance, a person who is mid-range on the fourth factor may be somewhat like the right-side Methodical; operating in a fairly organized manner and being goal oriented but they may also exhibit some traits from the left-side such as being flexible and not exhibiting a high attention to detail. It is much easier for a person in the mid-range to adjust behavior toward the right or left side than it is for a person clearly on one side to try and behave in a manner indicative of their mirror opposite side. To work like "the other side" – if you are on the right-side or left-side – requires energy and effort.

The midpoint of the continuum is the score of 50. Because of the bell curve and statistical probabilities, the lowest score possible for any given trait is 20 and the highest score is 80. The farther a person's score moves away from the mid-point of 50 the more intensely that trait is exhibited.

Trait intensity shown below is another important characteristic related to this type of graph. Note that as a score for a trait moves outward either left or right (+ or -) from the mid-point of 50 on the graph, the display of that behavioral trait for an individual becomes more intense. This is what we call Trait Intensity. Let's consider a single factor as an example:

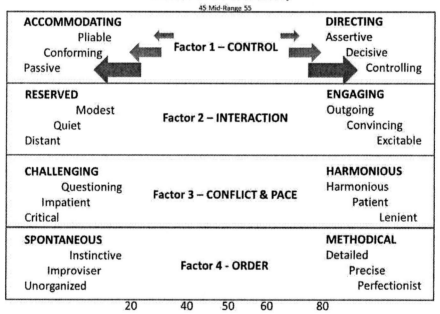

Path4 Factor 1: Control and Agenda

The Directing Side: As the score moves right from the mid-range score of 50 a person who is more Directing might display behavior that is Assertive (e.g. 57). Dial it up a notch due to stress and the trait intensifies to Decisive (60). If intensity goes even higher, the person's behavior may be labeled as controlling (65). The numbers for the scores are just approximate examples to help with illustration.

The Accommodating Side: On the opposite side of the continuum, a person whose score moves left from the mid-range score is Accommodating and might display behavior that makes them appear to be Pliable (44). Under stress that same behavior dialed up might be referred to as Conforming (35). Taken to the extreme, this person's behavior might be described as Passive (30). Again the numbers used here for the scores are just approximate examples for illustration.

Now that you have a basic understanding of how Path4 and Path6 measure hard-wired, natural behavior on a two sided continuum, let's talk about how to use the profiles responsibly. The following guidelines apply to RightPath Path4 and Path6 behavioral assessments. We are not necessarily like other products in the marketplace which may not be validated nor are they designed to remain stable over time and situation like the RightPath tools.

Guidelines for Using Path4 and Path6 Profiles.

1. **The profiles measure typical behaviors, i.e. normal behavioral traits.** The factors measured in Path4 and Path6 are designed to reveal recurring patterns of behaviors common to normal, healthy individuals. They are not psychological tools nor can they measure deviant behavior (Whew!).

2. **Individual's scores typically remain stable over time.** Although people can adapt to new situations and circumstances, most individuals revert to natural or "hard-wired" behaviors once the need to adapt is removed. While values, experience and knowledge can lead us to adapt natural behaviors on a more permanent basis, under stress, duress or deadline, natural tendencies typically override such

"learned" behaviors. This is a strong point of the RightPath tools versus other tools in the marketplace.

3. **Profiles and scores on the profiles are not "good" or "bad."** Every behavioral trait and every profile has its Strengths. The talents represented on opposing sides of the behavioral continuum are different, indeed, but they are equally important with their own corresponding list of Strengths and Struggles. Notice that RightPath tools are continuum-based tools – we don't believe in the "High" and "Low" concept that other tools may employ.

4. **Personal baggage is not identified by the profiles.** When someone is acting outside the boundaries of normal, socially accepted behavior, it is often a result of baggage such as a reaction to pain from the past or an overreaction due to past experiences. Since there is no such thing as the perfect life, we all carry some baggage with us. I once heard it said that a healthy person carries only enough baggage that he or she can safely stow over head or under the seat in front of them like on an airplane.

5. **The use of profiles should not lead to "putting a person in a box."** Using profiles to label individuals or put them in a 'behavioral box' is never a good idea. The complexity of human beings means that no two individuals are the same. Furthermore, people adapt and adjust based on environment and situations. Behavioral profiles are helpful in gaining understanding of individuals and their talents and they can even predict likely behavioral outcomes but they should never be used to label a person or restrict his or her development. RightPath works hard to avoid this pitfall. We want individuals to understand their uniqueness not to be conformed. We don't want our profiles to be used to *mold* people but rather to *unfold* them.

6. **Decisions should be made with a variety of input *not based solely on behavioral profiles*.** The insights provided by behavioral

assessments are powerful for decision-making but they are not meant to stand alone as a sole input – especially in selection. Other sources of information should be considered when making decisions related to people, whether for their work role or in their personal life. Some of the elements to take into consideration are current situational forces, a person's education, life experiences, background, and one's values. In selection, the application, references, background etc. – along with profile tools – make a good selection "tool kit."

7. **There is not a single profile that defines a leader.** In fact, leadership comes from any behavioral profile. The way a leader leads is affected by his or her behavioral profile, but all profiles can lead. The most important aspect of a person's leadership is his or her understanding of their own individual Strengths and Struggles and to use these to lead effectively. *A highly relational person will lead in a different manner than a detail-oriented introvert, but both possess talents (Strengths) that can be employed to make them exceptional leaders.* In a team session, I was once challenged on this concept. It caused me to go back and review my coaching clients over the past few years and it was confirmed. Of the sixteen blended profiles in Path4, I have personally worked with or coached a Fortune CEO with each of the profiles! However, they all learn to lead uniquely. Leadership can truly come from every profile!

With these foundational elements of behavioral assessments outlined, let's look at the four behavioral traits measured in the RightPath Path4 Profile. The following eight chapters outline each side of the profile's four traits – including typical Strengths, Struggles and tips for relating to people (at work or at home) who exhibit these traits and tendencies.

Coach's Notes:

As we prepare to unlock the specific keys to the specific behavioral traits, consider why objective information of this nature is helpful and what you hope to learn in the coming chapters.

What are you learning about your own behavioral preferences and development opportunities?

Record what you are discovering about how to optimize performance by understanding the behavioral talents of the people on your team.

CHAPTER 6

PATH4 – FACTOR 1
CONTROL
DIRECTING (RIGHT-SIDE)

Factor 1 - Control

Accommodating	Mid-Range	Directing

- Fit In
- Process-oriented
- Cooperative
- Cautious/Practical

- **Take Control**
- **Results-oriented**
- **Competitive**
- **Bold/Strategic**

The first factor of Path4 measures behavior as it relates to Control. This factor measures the drive to control the agenda and make decisions. People on the **right-side (Directing) are naturally motivated to take control** while individuals on the **left-side of the continuum (Accommodating) are naturally motivated to fit in.**

Starting with this chapter we will look at all four behavioral factors of Path4 by looking first at the right-hand side of the trait and then at the left-hand side. Remember that both sides of the continuum have Strengths or talents (natural behavioral tendencies which can be productively applied) as well as the "two-sided coin" of Struggles. And, the Mid-Range (i.e. scores between 45 and 55) area indicates flexibility for an individual in this or any factor. Mid-Range also means this is not a key trait for that person. Someone with scores in this area will be able to more easily adapt especially if influenced by the situation they are in. They will tend to operate with a blend of traits from either side of the continuum. People in the Mid-Range will likely identify with strengths and struggles from both sides of the behavioral factor.

Let's start by looking at the right-side of Factor 1 – **Directing.** If you have taken Path4 online, great! You will know whether your score is left-side (44 or less), Mid-Range (45 to 55) or right-side (56+). If not, in each chapter you can use the descriptive diagram for each factor at the beginning and end of each chapter as a place to mark on the continuum where you believe your natural behavioral talents fall for this factor. If you aren't sure which side your score would be on because you exhibit traits from both sides, your score may likely be in the Mid-Range.

Factor 1 - Control

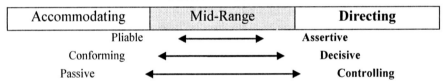

Accommodating	Mid-Range	**Directing**

Pliable		**Assertive**
Conforming		**Decisive**
Passive		**Controlling**

Individuals who score on the right-side (56 or higher) of this trait are **Directing**. These individuals are naturally driven to control their environment. Comfortable giving directions to others, directing individuals naturally assume authority. They are results-oriented, self-assured and often express opinions in a strong and direct manner.

Although individuals with Directing traits are often outspoken, it is a myth or common misconception to assume that, based on their vocal nature, they are necessarily extroverts. Communication for a person who exhibits Directing traits is for a purpose and if an individual has strong verbal skills, they may seem more outgoing than they really are. Highly directing people are more often introverts than extroverts.

The Strengths and Struggles associated with the right side behavioral traits for this factor – Directing – are listed below. Notice that the Struggles are often correlated to the Strengths but they are often taken to the extreme where the behavior becomes ineffective (over-done).

DIRECTING TRAIT

Strengths:	Struggles:
• Initiating, wants to set the agenda	• Opinionated; discounts input from others
• Results-oriented	• May be controlling and not know it
• Speaks directly	• Typically not good at listening
• Competitive, takes on challenges	• Prefers to avoid routine and details
• Prefers multiple projects	• Underestimates work needed to achieve goals
• Sees the strategic/future potential	• May over-commit what others can do

DIRECTING STRENGTHS

People Who Possess Talents in the Area of Directing Behavioral Traits are Typically Results-Oriented.

Directing individuals like to initiate action, get things done and move quickly. They are decisive. They are able to push ideas into reality with their strong will and driving nature. It is difficult for these individuals not to be in charge or take charge. They may disengage or seek other challenges if they feel like they are not part of the action. Getting results is paramount to them.

Descriptors of these individuals would include words such as **daring, confident, driving, bold, and assertive.** They naturally assume their solutions are sound and will be the best way to get things done. Obstacles do not deter them; rather they are driven to overcome them. If a task is labeled impossible or too difficult, they will rise to the challenge to try to prove the nay-sayers wrong. Even at times when they are not in control, they may think they are, act as if they are, or may be certain that it is only a matter of time until the steering wheel is back in their hands. Giving up control is very difficult for Directing individuals.

With quick working minds, people with Directing Strengths often enjoy a fast pace and require multiple projects to keep them engaged. Their opinions are seldom mild and they like to look out to the future with strategic vision for what a finished project will accomplish or what a completed product will look like.

The need for control is linked closely to the need to be right and the tendency to be opinionated. You seldom have to guess what a Directing person is thinking. They will tell you and often in a blunt or at least direct manner. They are often described as commanding, assured and confident.

Their confidence is strongest when they have the reins. Feeling more secure in their own ability to lead, they trust themselves and their judgment, and tend to be skeptical of others. Directing personalities often have a solid understanding and "read" of power structures and they use power as a means of protecting their turf. If they cannot determine that someone holds the power in a situation or environment, they will quickly step up to fill it with their own influence.

The need for power goes hand in hand with a Directing individual's competitive drive and desire to come out on top. Winning is the desired outcome for these highly assertive individuals and even in the face of impending defeat they are slow to wave the white flag. They will exhaust all avenues in an effort to get the results they desire. While other behavioral traits can demonstrate competitiveness, the need to win is very serious for this group. Key Strengths for this trait include producing Results and being decisive.

DIRECTING STRUGGLES

Feedback stings but it is necessary for development with all factors. For the Directing trait, as for all the others, most Struggles are not related to things this person cannot do. Rather, they often take their positive talents to the extreme, which becomes unproductive. In this case, a Directing person may move from being in control and self-assured to the Struggle side of being **egotistical, self-centered,** and **insensitive** to others. Ego can motivate a person to succeed, but it also can become one's undoing when taken too far.

If you were to ask a Directing person what is great about this trait, they might tell you that he is the one who gets things done by telling others what to do. Or that she is the one who makes up her mind and then puts people into motion with her plan. Those on the receiving end of the Directing person's orders however might tell you that these individuals can become bossy, impatient, poor listeners, controlling, self-centered and overly opinionated. The most frequently seen manifestation of this trait is poor listening skills.

When a Directing person's positive traits are over-done (turning into Struggles that cause irritation to those around them), it is often an issue of ego. Shifting focus from self to others will help a Directing person to reign in the urge to over-control. They can learn to observe others as they operate and notice or read when reactions might indicate they are steam rolling rather than leading those in their charge. Honest feedback sought from friends or confidants can also help these highly driven people to recognize when their Strengths are being over-employed and are negatively affecting others.

Decisiveness is the hallmark of a Directing person's mode of operation. Many who possess Directing Strengths have a solid track record of success and high confidence level. These Strengths and success markers can cause a person to believe they are **always right** – even though that's simply not possible for any human. We all know that no person is right all the time! But, if a person believes they are right even *most* of the time – they can be resistant in accepting other viewpoints or ways of thinking. They tend to shoot the messenger rather than accept negative feedback or challenges to their thought process. However, learning to accept such challenging and feedback can be the very thing that such leaders need to move to the next level of development and success – they may need to be proven wrong in order to move on.

If a Directing individual is convinced that his or her way is right at all costs, you will usually find them unwilling to be challenged. This is where the four D's may kick in. They will *deny* what is being suggested. They will *defend* their position and solution. They may even *demonize* those who challenge them and in the most extreme cases even try to *destroy* their opposition. Obviously, this example goes to the extreme but that's the point – Struggles are often Strengths over-done and taken to the extreme. Because the start of such a progression is Strength – and perhaps one that the leader relies heavily on – helping the individual see where this trait becomes counter-productive or even destructive can be difficult. It is their natural "go to" trait.

So, what is the antidote to always needing to be right? Humility. Directing individuals need to see that they are not perfect – they can and will make mistakes. They are wrong at times and they need to learn not only to consider but to value the input of others around them. It is not weakness but Strength that allows a leader to move from pride to humility and show concern for others.

Often people with strong Directing talents admit that they are **not great listeners.** Their need to be in charge can cause their thoughts to race ahead before fully hearing what others have to say. High confidence, especially when backed by a successful track record, can further impair a Directing leader's ability to listen.

Listening to others takes time and Directing people covet their time fiercely and maximize its use. Sometimes they are simply too impatient to listen because they have other things pressing on their agenda. They want to move fast. Stopping to listen impairs their flow and often includes uncertainty as to how long it will take to hear out the other person. Quick moving minds fast-forward to their response before the person's input is completely received (incomplete listening) particularly if they disagree with that input.

On a positive note, while developing good listening skills is a challenge – Directing individuals love a challenge! We have found that employing various practices allows the Directing individual to disengage from multi-tasking and it helps them to listen better. One leader I coach employs a technique where he puts down his smartphone or turns away from his computer before he verbally acknowledges the other person. He also verbalizes his willingness to hear what they have to say, which has become a cue to help him to better engage his listening skills. I encouraged another Directing individual to jot down a few notes – especially when listening to things she has strong opinions about. This frees her mind up to focus on the rest of what the speaker has to say, rather than to be preoccupied with crafting her rebuttal. We coach Directing leaders that preparing your response is not a form of listening! Loading your guns does not create a dialog. Mentally preparing the list of how someone is wrong in the middle of the conversation doesn't count as listening!

Practice and patience are the keys to becoming a better listener – and reading body language also is significant. Many individuals admit that it is within their family relationships that they are more likely to be pressed to learn to listen better and to become more relationally aware and engaged.

IDEAL WORK ENVIRONMENT

Directing people work best when they can build, direct, develop, create, lead, conceptualize, decide, control, and initiate solutions.

Directing Personalities Don't Like To Be Managed.

Individuals who are Directing need to have control. They need turf that is their own and clear boundaries. With challenging goals, sufficient resources and freedom to operate, they will succeed and get results.

While this group of individuals is good at getting results, they can be a challenge to manage. They are assertive enough to press through roadblocks and cut red tape. And they're brave enough to jump ship if they don't like the vessel they are on. Boundaries are not always easy to enforce because they naturally hunger for turf, power and control. If those people leading these Directing individuals are not strong, these people might roll right over them too, or at least roll around them!

Directing individuals appreciate direct communication. Anticipate that they will try to overstep boundaries en route to their goals and when they do, act quickly to get their attention and redirect as necessary. These people understand clear and direct better than subtle and diplomatic. If you ask them subtly to do something or worse yet stop doing something, they will know the power is theirs. Decisive, swift leadership communicated very directly is key in keeping Directing individuals on track to success without too much peripheral damage. This Directing factor is wired to test all boundaries.

Factor 1 - Control

Accommodating	Mid-Range	**Directing**

Motivated to

FIT IN ◄─────────────► TAKE CONTROL

If you have not taken the RightPath Path4 online, consider the graphic above. Based on the information you have just read, do you believe you would score on the right-side, or Directing side, of this trait? If so, mark an X on the graphic by Directing. The next chapter will help you identify whether you might be on the left-side (Accommodating) or Mid-Range section of this trait.

If you would like to take RightPath Path4 and Path6 profiles online, see Page 205 for instructions or visit www.rightpath.com.

Coach's Notes:

If you are Directing…

If you are working with or leading a person who is Directing…

CHAPTER 7

PATH4 – FACTOR 1
CONTROL
ACCOMMODATING (LEFT-SIDE)

Factor 1 - Control

Accommodating	Mid-Range	Directing

▪ **Fit In**	▪ Take Control
▪ **Process-oriented**	▪ Results-oriented
▪ **Cooperative**	▪ Competitive
▪ **Cautious/Practical**	▪ Bold/Strategic

In the last chapter we looked at the right-side of this factor, now we will consider the left-side. People on the **Accommodating side of the continuum for the Control factor are naturally motivated to fit in.** Typically, pleased to work in team-oriented environments, these individuals are cooperative and tend to be both collaborative and process-oriented. They are an integral part of the organization's success because they are adept at implementing the plans, strategies and vision once they are devised and set.

55

Factor 1 - Control

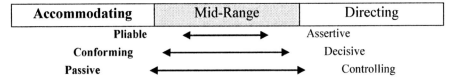

Accommodating	Mid-Range	Directing

Pliable	Assertive
Conforming	Decisive
Passive	Controlling

Strengths and Struggles for the Accommodating[7] traits are naturally opposite from those of the Directing side of the trait. Accommodating individuals do not need to take control but rather, they desire to fit in and desire to support the established agenda.

ACCOMMODATING TRAIT

Strengths:	**Struggles:**
• Loyal, follows the set agenda	• Can be unassertive, timid
• Process-oriented	• May tend towards being passive
• Speaks tactfully	• May be hesitant to speak out
• Cooperative – promotes stability	• May avoid taking charge
• Moves cautiously into new areas	• Tends to underestimate self
• Focused – likes to do one thing at a time	• May agree, then regret or resent it
• Sees the practical for here and now	• May lack strategic vision

ACCOMMODATING STRENGTHS

Cooperation and collaboration are the name of the game for Accommodating individuals. They enjoy being part of a team and like to follow a set agenda. Loyalty typically runs high in this group of people and they like helping others to be successful. These personalities are likeable, persuasive but not overbearing and are seen as team players.

Individuals who are strong in this trait do not have the ego need to leave their unique mark on projects. They are usually process-oriented and can see the practical elements of projects. Skilled at maintaining or operating a program that is already established, they may shy away from

---

[7] From RightPath® Path4 Profile

implementing brand new processes and may not naturally suggest pioneering a brand new process from scratch.

They focus on the practical and what is happening today. Able to sort through details, they are great at executing a plan but may struggle with visionary abilities beyond the process or project at hand. They lend a realistic and practical voice to their team and its work.

Individuals with Strengths from the Accommodating trait tend to be more than just good team players. They also tend to be **diplomatic, speak tactfully and promote stability and cooperation.** Given the chance, they would usually prefer to cooperate than engage in conflict until all other options are exhausted. They often contribute to a sense of calm and tend to be well liked by peers and leaders alike. They also are adept at mediation, building consensus, and bridge building.

Accommodating individuals are usually relational. Leaders with these traits use their **Relationship-orientation** as a platform from which to lead. Naturally humble, they often do not care who gets the credit so long as the job is well done, processes run smoothly and success is achieved. They are the sort of leader that people like to fall in step behind. In leadership sessions, time after time, we hear the same thing when people are asked about the greatest leader they have ever experienced. They are humble, approachable, gracious, self-effacing, relational, and good listeners. In virtually every team session we conduct, the participants list relational qualities – those familiar to many Accommodating individuals – as some of the traits that define their best leaders as great.

Relationship-Oriented Leaders Can Still Get Results. That is perhaps the most important thing to remember as we wrap up the strengths related to this relational trait called Accommodating. It is a misconception that these leaders can't get Results. With good learned behavior, they can do it. Being Accommodating doesn't mean they cannot be Directing – they can. They will tend to move to Directing actions only when required or when they are passionate about an issue.

Good Relationships motivate individuals leading to desired Results.

ACCOMMODATING STRUGGLES

Humility over-done can appear to others as a lack of confidence, unwillingness to speak out or timidity. Because individuals with Accommodating strengths do not crave the limelight or accolades, they can at times be seen as individuals who are passive or who lack the confidence to take charge.

Accommodating individuals often have **a tendency to second guess their capability** – even if they are in fact well prepared, suitably skilled and intelligent. Because of their collaborative orientation, they may be uncomfortable when it comes to risk taking or pressing their ideas especially when others' ideas are already on the table. Often the provision of regular feedback and learned behavior can help to assure them that they are on track and counter balance their hesitation. On a team with strong Directing personalities however, they will need significant encouragement to speak up as they may naturally lean towards diplomacy and even silence once the noise starts around them.

Confidence in self, awareness of their skills and their value to the team can help Accommodating people to speak up. The discomfort or the hesitating to speak out will be more easily overcome when it is a topic or an issue the Accommodating individual is passionate about. This means they will tend to choose their battles carefully.

Concerned about details and keeping the peace, Accommodating individuals often hesitate to immediately step forward with a decision, preferring first to secure buy-in from everyone else. While consensus is a good thing, when timeliness matters more, this tendency can delay action, cause missed deadlines and impedes timely results. Indecisiveness and too much discussion can be the result of too many meetings and cause secondary issues like a loss of momentum for the project or goals at hand.

Increasing an individual's confidence and encouraging risk

taking can help an Accommodating person to overcome these Struggles. It is also advantageous to assign an experienced mentor or coach and who is at least Mid-Range in this Factor and appreciates Accommodating virtues. The mentor can provide insights for an Accommodating individual's development. And since the mentor is not a polar opposite from the person he or she is assigned to − the mentor and can likely provide insights for development and help identify ways to improve this person's challenges. This sort of relationship, particularly to an Accommodating person, gives them a safe place and sense of collaboration as well as an opportunity to grow, build confidence, gain knowledge and succeed.

Because Accommodating individuals are typically process-oriented, they may **lack longer-term strategic vision**. While they can look for kinks in the system and plan out projects, they are often so practical that it is hard to think long-term or look past current technology. They are less interested in vision, trends and possibilities than the day-to-day that needs attention now.

How does an Accommodating individual learn to develop strategic vision and the ability to look at the bigger picture?

Learning about current trends in their industry or environment helps. Adding new information sources to the menu from which they operate can also bring a new, broader perspective to their thinking. They can also learn to pay attention to the visionaries in their organization, or gain exposure to other organizations; and learn from them.

IDEAL WORK ENVIRONMENT

People who are Accommodating work best when the goals and vision are clearly defined and there is a consistent work process. They are usually more productive when their tasks focus on maintaining, rather than initiating.

As natural team players, Accommodating personalities are easy to manage for the most part because they are collaborative and well, accommodating. You can bring out the best in them by encouraging them to express their ideas, by asking them questions and by listening to what they have to say. They may need some reassurance that you really do want to hear their true opinion on a matter. As leaders themselves, they are great at thinking about their team, and they will care whether or not they are liked by those who work for them. When leading an Accommodating individual who is leading others, encourage that person to initiate action, take risks and not be afraid to make tough decisions.

Defining Mid-Range

Scores in any trait that fall on or between 45 and 55 are called mid-range. One third of the general population will fall in the mid-range for each behavioral trait. Individuals with mid-range scores will exhibit Strengths and Struggles from either side of the behavioral trait. However, the display of the tendencies of the factor for which the score is mid-range will not play out as intensely as they do for individuals whose scores appear clearly on the right-side or the left-side.

What if I am in the middle? What if I am neither clearly Directing nor Accommodating?

A third of the population falls on the right-side of each behavioral trait (in this case - Directing), a third falls on the left side (in this case - Accommodating) and the final one third falls in the Mid-Range. The third of the population that falls in the Mid-Range exhibits Strengths or talents from both the right and the left side of this factor. Because the behavior is not so extreme, their display of the talents on the Accommodating – Directing continuum will be more muted and less intense, and also less likely to exhibit the resulting Struggles when the behavioral traits of this factor are overplayed.

Factor 1 - Control

Accommodating	Mid-Range	Directing

Motivated to

FIT IN ◄━━━━━━━━► TAKE CONTROL

A person who is Mid-Range can lead at times and follow at times. They may assert themselves in the absence of another leader stepping up to take charge or may be content to follow the lead of a competent person who has taken the steering wheel on a project or team. It is much easier for these individuals in the Mid-Range to adjust to either side of the factor than it is for a person who is clearly on the right-side to move to the left, or for one who is clearly on the left-side to move to the right.

If you have not taken Path4 online, consider the graphic above. Based on the information you have just read, do you believe you would score on the left-side, or Accommodating side, of this trait? If so, mark an X on the graphic by Accommodating. Or, if you possess a blend of the talents from both sides, mark an X in the Mid-Range section for this trait to show that you have Strengths and Struggles from both sides of this factor.

If you would like to take RightPath Path4 and Path6 profiles online, see Page 205 for instructions or visit www.rightpath.com.

Coach's Notes:

If you are Accommodating…

If you are working with or leading a person who is Accommodating…

CHAPTER 8

PATH4 – FACTOR 2
INTERACTION
ENGAGING (RIGHT-SIDE)

Factor 2 - Interaction

Reserved	Mid-Range	**Engaging**

- Reflect
- Avoid Attention
- Serious
- Realistic

- **Express**
- **Gain Recognition**
- **Humorous**
- **Optimistic**

The second factor reported in the Path4 report measures behavior as it relates to **Interaction**. This factor indicates a person's openness in expression, transparency, and ease in relating to strangers. People on the **right-side (Engaging) are naturally motivated to gain attention and express themselves** and individuals on the **left-side of the continuum (Reserved) are naturally motivated to avoid attention and reflect**.

Factor 2 - Interaction

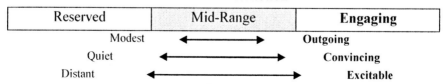

Reserved	Mid-Range	**Engaging**
Modest	←————→	**Outgoing**
Quiet	←————————→	**Convincing**
Distant	←——————————→	**Excitable**

Interaction is much as its name suggests – this factor displays how an individual tends to interact with others. This factor in Path4 is unique because it is not a measurement of Extroversion (see Chapter 18 for our measure of true Extroversion via Path6). This profile does not measure pure extroversion (someone who is energized by engaging with people) and introversion (someone who is fatigued by engagement with people, particularly strangers). Rather it measure's a person's ability and willingness to engage in communication, conversation and social interaction for a purpose. This factor, Interaction, measures a person's ability, ease, and enjoyment related to engaging an audience (regardless of size) and interfacing with people.

Those on the right-side of this factor, Engaging individuals, typically enjoy time spent with other people. Particularly if they have a topic they are passionate about, they will strike up conversations with friends and strangers alike. For highly Engaging people, the person who sits next to them on an airplane is not a nuisance but an opportunity to engage.

Most Engaging people are pretty easy to spot. When speaking before a group, they seem comfortable, not fidgety. If they're not offered a spot in the limelight they might just make a way there themselves. They are talkative and enthusiastic particularly if they are working on a project they are passionate about or are speaking about themselves. One way to tell if a person is **Engaging *and* Extroverted** or just Engaging is to see whether they seem more or less energized after spending a significant length of time interacting with a group of people. If the Engaging person is also truly Extroverted, they will seem energized and seek out people to talk to even after they have spent a full day with people. The Engaging and Extroverted person doesn't tire of people and seeks frequent opportunities to connect with individuals. However, if an Engaging person is not also Extroverted, he or she will tend to engage for the purpose at hand, answer questions and pursue conversations – but will disengage when the conversations are completed and may seem somewhat fatigued when the time of interaction is over. This person is able to engage their audience but then will need time away from interaction and people contact to recharge their batteries and fully re-energize. This can present significant coaching implications.

ENGAGING TRAIT

Strengths:	Struggles:
• Good at meeting strangers	• Strong need for approval of others
• Light-hearted and enthusiastic	• May talk too much
• Optimistic	• Tends to be overly optimistic
• Enjoys being in the spotlight	• May lack focus
• Good at promoting	• May display strong emotion
• Likes to make a good impression	• May be too transparent, too uninhibited
• Likes open-ended situations	• Usually not good at working alone

ENGAGING STRENGTHS

Engaging individuals are driven to relate to others. They are outwardly focused and like to share their thoughts and opinions. Their best thinking is done as they talk; verbalizing is part of how they process. While quieter individuals may find it hard to believe, often the Engaging person may not know what is coming out of their mouth until it has been said. In coaching, I refer to this as "verbal white-boarding." This instinctive, impromptu edge is a key part of this factor.

Recognition, admiration and popularity are common drives for the Engaging individual. The need to be acknowledged drives them toward social interaction and relationships. The desire to engage is heightened when this person is passionate about a cause or project and the "cause" or purpose drives their interaction. Too much time on their own can be extremely frustrating to Engaging individuals.

There is one group of people, this need for interaction is often extremely high – teenagers. Teens often become more social and have a high need for interaction as they go through adolescence. The importance of friends and fun increases and youth often exhibit Engaging traits more during this phase of life than at other times. Once past the teen years however, research finds that individuals tend to settle back into their normal tendency, even if temporarily inflated during their pubescent development period.

And finally, Engaging individuals with a very high amount of public exposure may find their natural desire to interact gets a bit weary. Often public figures are Engaging in relation to a cause or project they are passionate about and thus people can tend to stretch themselves in this factor. And, after a large amount of interaction these people need downtime to recharge and re-energize before they can effectively reengage.

If you want someone to greet and welcome people at a social function, or someone to host the international group that is coming to town, then look first to this group. Engaging individuals smile easily, and they are also genuine in their **enthusiasm for strangers**. All of their talents collectively enable them to make **good first impressions**.

Openness is an important asset attributed to this group. They tend to be transparent and willing to share their inner thoughts openly with others. Engaging people have an openness to receive others into their circle of friends and are often open to new ideas as well as new people. Because they like to dialog, they often like to brainstorm and be a part of creative processes, but the key is for them is to be with others.

Optimistic by nature, these individuals see the brighter side of life and tend to assume the best in most circumstances and situations. The **upbeat,** Engaging individual is often **good at promoting** ideas, other people and themselves. Their enthusiasm is contagious and they use emotion to their advantage to engage others in their dialog. At a party you can spot this person because they are surrounded by people, the dialog is lively and there's likely a good bit of laughter in the mix.

Engaging people like to talk. Highly Engaging people love to talk. Strong verbal communication skills are among the most evident of an Engaging person's Strengths. They do not waste an opportunity to tell you their opinion or promote their agenda. These are the people you want to have as your "front man" or spokesperson for bringing attention to a project, cause or product being sold. In the "Tipping Point" concept, they are your mavens.

ENGAGING STRUGGLES

Working alone can be difficult for Engaging individuals. Working with others is much more fun than shutting the door and working solo on a project. Ideas flow better when they talk them out with others but at some point, most jobs require an Engaging person to buckle down and get things done. Procrastination can come into play – especially if the person is dreading the time away from interaction in order to get a task or project done. They can easily get weary from their solo, focused work.

While you can expect some procrastination from Engaging individuals, you can also expect that once they are working they will be like a whirlwind, trying to get things done. This is partially because they delayed getting started, but it's also because they tend to be **overly optimistic** regarding the time it will take for completion. An Engaging individual's sunny disposition leads them to often underestimate the amount of time and work required to meet deadlines. They are often people pleasers who are quick to say "Yes" to projects, but a smart manager will remember they lean towards being overly optimistic. To avoid missing the mark on projects, try touching base with these individuals along the way to see whether things are on track or not. The good news is that these individuals have lots of friends they can call in at the last minute to help with meeting a looming deadline. Learning to rely on a day planner, calendar and tracking time on projects can help to avoid missing deadlines. It also lets the Engaging person see in writing how much time it really takes to accomplish the tasks at hand. These skills allow Engaging individuals to develop their own personal work system. It is also helpful to ask someone more methodical to help set or validate a realistic timeline on projects.

Talking too much is a common Struggle for Engaging individuals. Employing good observation skills can help these people to recognize when this is happening. We all need to learn to read cues during interaction with others so we can communicate effectively with them. This ability, however, is helpful to an Engaging person because it assists in teaching him or her to recognize when it is time to dial back the dialog. For instance, if the person you are talking to starts looking at their watch, fiddling with their pen, shifting in their chair, or giving fewer verbal or facial responses to what is being said, chances are they are ready to move on. Or, if the person listening leans forward and tries to interject as the Engaging person speaks, that means they've heard enough and may have a question or comment to include in the dialog.

Individuals who are Engaging often have a hard time saying, "No." When opportunities come along, especially those involving people they like, they do not want to miss out on the fun. This means they can often find themselves **over committed, overwhelmed and struggling with focus.** Eager to try new things and being open to others and their ideas, Engaging individuals sometimes find they have more "spinning plates" to keep balanced and in the air than they bargained for. One of the dangers of being overloaded is that attention to detail can quickly fade as they try to keep their heads above water and promises or deadlines slip away. The quality of work they want to exhibit can also be diminished as part of this downward spiral.

The key to helping Engaging people avoid being overcommitted and overwhelmed lies in three elements: prioritization, focus and learning to say "No." Asking a supervisor, trusted peer, or coach to help prioritize projects is a must – just like learning to keep a calendar and use planning tools.

In addition to being open, Engaging individuals often exhibit behavior that tends to be **uninhibited or emotional** in nature. Being quick to speak and having a high need to relate to people can sometimes cause issues. While disagreements in the work place and home life are perfectly normal, Engaging people may tend to take differences of opinion very personally. Being open, approachable and uninhibited can make it very easy for people to relate to them, it can also make it hard for them to mask their own emotions whether positive or negative. If an Engaging person wants to hide something that is bothering him or her, the greatest chance for success lies in the ability to hold their tongue. The verbal/emotional combination can be a challenge.

If an Engaging person has a strong opinion about something, good or bad, once they open their mouth you will usually know exactly what they are thinking. The key to not reacting with too much emotion and not speaking too quickly is the practice of "reading" situations combined with self-control. It's a good idea to coach Engaging individuals to "count to ten" to delay their response or to question before speaking in a situation where emotions are running high. It is also helpful for them to learn to make a quick mental assessment of who is present in the room and the potential impact of their words – to help them consider the broader ramifications of what they say, and as a part of "reading" the situation.

What if it is too late and the words are out there or the Engaging person has spoken emotionally or overreacted in front of a superior or a friend? The good news is that others likely know the relational wiring of the person who made the comments. While they might be surprised if a shy person speaks up sharply, an Engaging person is known for speaking up.

When coaching an Engaging individual in struggle areas such as conflict or having a hasty or sharp tongue, it is beneficial to remind them to de-personalize the conflict. Help them to see the bigger picture rather than assessing the situation as a personal attack. Often, just having a trusted person to vent to, one who can absorb some of the emotion, is the best remedy. Once the dust settles after a conflict or when boundaries have been crossed, a note or letter of apology is often a good fix to start the process of mending fences. Writing an apology rather than giving it verbally allows the recipient time to fully process the words. It and also gives more time for the emotion to settle down and tone to change. Later, an in-person apology is appropriate.

Direct communication from an Engaging person is a good Strength, in the right measure and at the right time. The key is to learn to manage the tendencies to say too much, too quickly and to over-personalize interactions with others.

IDEAL WORK ENVIRONMENT

A fast-paced, fun environment with lots of interaction with people is a great work environment for Engaging people. With a need for variety and mobility in their daily routine, these individuals often choose careers where they can influence, impact, train, or encourage others. Opportunities which employ their enthusiasm and strong verbal skills give them a chance to shine and ramps up personal fulfillment and satisfaction.

Because they are so relational, **managing Engaging individuals involves being relational.** They need work which uses their people skills and they need lots of feedback along the way. Even if it is obvious to you as a manager that they are doing a good job, give encouraging feedback anyway. They need it. Make time in your day to listen to what these people have to say and try to remember that they aren't just talking – they are thinking and analyzing as they talk. Avoid the urge to analyze every word that comes out of their mouths. Instead see where the conversation ends up once they have finished the verbal processing. Remember, they are using talking like a "verbal whiteboard."

Solitary tasks and those requiring great focus will be hardest for

Engaging individuals. Assistance and encouragement as they try to stay focused is helpful. Hold them accountable and schedule meetings to track progress, assess challenges and review priorities. They will appreciate both the face time such meetings afford and the accountability too.

As with every trait, the Struggles outlined for Engaging individuals are the flipside of their Strengths. Because this group of people is open and approachable, adding a little fun into personal development often works too. Humor can take the sting out of constructive criticism and once again, encouragement is always appreciated as they make progress in their Struggles.

Factor 2 - Interaction

Reserved	Mid-Range	Engaging

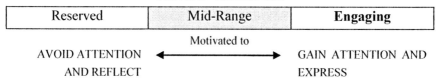

AVOID ATTENTION AND REFLECT ← Motivated to → GAIN ATTENTION AND EXPRESS

If you have not taken Path4 online, consider the graphic above. Based on the information you have just read, do you believe you would score on the right-side, or Engaging side, of this trait? If so, mark an X on the graphic by Engaging. If the information in this chapter didn't seem to fit you, your score is likely on the left-side (Reserved) or Mid-Range. Read on to the next chapter to see which fits you best.

If you would like to take RightPath Path4 and Path6 profiles online, see Page 205 for instructions or visit www.rightpath.com.

Coach's Notes:

If you are Engaging...

If you are working with or leading a person who is Engaging...

CHAPTER 9

PATH4 – FACTOR 2
INTERACTION
RESERVED (LEFT-SIDE)

Factor 2 - Interaction

Reserved	Mid-Range	Engaging

- **Reflect**
- **Avoid Attention**
- **Serious**
- **Realistic**

- Express
- Gain Recognition
- Humorous
- Optimistic

The left-side of the Interaction continuum is called **Reserved.** While it is not hard to think of what the opposite of an Engaging individual is, understanding this "quieter" side is not always so easy – particularly for those who are wired to be more Engaging. To spot the Reserved people in a room, shift your focus. Instead of looking for the ones trying to gain your attention, look for those who are deflecting attention, who are listening rather than talking, who are processing rather than verbalizing. Notice the people taking notes or quietly reflecting rather than interjecting in the conversation at hand.

Factor 2 - Interaction

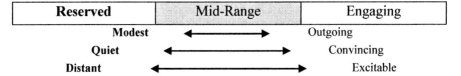

Reserved	Mid-Range	Engaging

Modest	← →	Outgoing
Quiet	← →	Convincing
Distant	← →	Excitable

Reserved individuals often marvel at the amount of information their chatty counterparts are willing to put out on public display. They are far more private in most cases, particularly with personal information. Even reading through this segment may feel like exposure to them because we are discussing traits that tell about how they think and who they are, and that rarely gets revealed!

RESERVED TRAIT

Strengths:	Struggles:
• Task-oriented	• May appear withdrawn and aloof
• Serious and modest	• Sometimes come across as shy
• Realistic and practical	• Tends to be pessimistic
• Has a dry sense of humor	• Can be curt
• Good at persevering	• May seem quietly self-righteous
• Likes to be focused	• May appear skeptical or secretive
• Likes closure	• Typically drained by social contact

Reserved people don't seek public attention or fame but sometimes it finds them. Although they do not like to be in the spotlight, sometimes they have to be. It is not that a Reserved person cannot communicate; they can. However, they are accepting of someone else taking that role instead or they prefer to communicate in a pace or manner that *they* choose – not one that someone else chooses for them.

RESERVED STRENGTHS

Reserved individuals are **task-oriented** versus relationally-oriented. Free from distractions of what others are thinking or what other people are doing, they like to focus and settle into the work at hand.

They often pride themselves on and enjoy taking very few words to say what needs to be said.

Finishing what they start, staying focused and closure matter to Reserved individuals. Thus, they are often happy working alone with very little or limited interaction with other people. It is not that they don't like people, but rather they do not like interruptions and distractions others often bring. Interaction is fine when they want to talk, but it's not acceptable when they are focused on the task at hand and the required work they have to do.

Reserved people typically process information internally and this makes them **quiet, reflective and deliberate.** They do not need to express every thought they have, preferring to mull over and think through their thoughts and ideas. When posed with a problem or situation, their immediate response is usually, "Let me think it over." And, they will. The Reserved person will think about the problem or issue, formulate a response and deliver it in a well thought out, logical, reasoned manner – not in an immediate response like Engaging people tend to do.

Reserved individuals resist the urge to give an immediate answer, preferring to reflect and process information before responding. While this trait can be frustrating for their Engaging counter parts; those wise enough will learn that waiting and giving the Reserved person time to process will afford them a much better reply when that person finally is ready to respond.

At times these individuals may be considered low key because they are typically quiet. They might also be described as **realistic, to-the-point and unemotional.** When their reply does arrive, it is typically void of excess words and also void of unnecessary emotion. Reserved people are a matter-of-fact bunch and as you might expect because they choose their words carefully and speak fewer of them, they often avoid verbal conflict. They tell it like it is and take pride in delivering facts swiftly and concisely when they are ready.

Reserved people tend to be **realistic in giving appraisals and making commitments**. They tend to be conservative in estimations, not wanting to overstate or understate what is required for a project or job. They would rather decline a project than over-commit and miss the mark. I once worked with a group of engineers who did this well. At first their conservative responses frustrated me but after completing two projects with them, I had figured out their number. They would downplay their abilities and capabilities. These individuals would always under-commit and over-perform.

RESERVED STRUGGLES

The Reserved person may be seen as **unfriendly or aloof.** Because they are not fans of social contact, they can seem closed to others particularly if the 'others' are a group of strangers.

No matter the role, for most jobs, some socializing or at least socialization is necessary. Reserved people can adapt to these requirements and even become quite good at it. It may never feel comfortable but when interacting with others is necessary for work, or is required to keep a project moving, or is fueled by something a Reserved individual is passionate about, it is worth the discomfort. At first the Reserved individual may dislike what may feel like being "phony" but once they realize they are really just adapting their behavior out of necessity rather than "faking it" it is easier to encourage this behavior. When they realize they have to engage to further their passion, it gets easier over time.

An interesting phenomenon with Reserved individuals is that they often don't see themselves as being as Reserved as they are because they can be social with others – that is, with others they get to know well. Because they become comfortable with people they know well, Reserved people may not accurately see how distant they can appear around strangers or people they don't know, including co-workers.

When we look at Path6 we will discuss the difference between simply being Reserved and being a true Introvert. Suffice to say here that **true Introverts are drained by interaction with people**. They need time away from other people to recharge their batteries. It is more than just a matter of preferring one-on-one interaction to a crowd or preferring to be quiet rather than speak up. An introvert is Reserved as measured in Path4 and also needs off-line, alone time to process and renew/recharge their energy.

Reserved individuals whose roles grow to include more and more meetings and interaction can find the added time with people to be very stressful. This becomes a true development issue for leaders climbing the ladder. *If you are a Reserved person and feel your stress levels rising, consider if you have had enough downtime, on your own, to process and recharge. Too many meetings scheduled too tightly will wear you out. I coach Reserved executives that it might be time to schedule a meeting or two with yourself to regain your sense of balance.*

The Reserved person may be viewed as **pessimistic, closed-minded, or unenthusiastic,** particularly if seen through the eyes of a person who is the optimistic, Engaging sort. Reserved people are wise to keep watch on their tendency towards pessimism and try to keep the bigger picture in mind instead of focusing only on the detours and obstacles. This occurs because Reserved people, by reflecting, can often see potential problems and pitfalls earlier than others. If the environment is highly charged and enthusiastic, the Reserved person may struggle with the urge to respond with the polar opposite view rather than trying to meet the eager beavers half way to find workable solutions that include a healthy sense of balance.

The Reserved person is in many cases valued for this natural skepticism and realistic approach. The key to keeping this Strength from becoming a hindrance in a team environment is to weigh their viewpoint with the overall need of the organization and team to make progress. Just because you can see a pitfall doesn't mean it will always occur!

Isolating themselves and being slow to respond or

incommunicative are also common tendencies of Reserved individuals. Being isolated from a group often does not bother them, and when coupled with body language that is closed (such as crossed arms or sitting pushed back/away), people around them are often more comfortable leaving the Reserved individuals in their isolation. This sort of behavior, however, is highly detrimental to productive teamwork. Coaxing them to share information and opinions is often met with resistance, but it is the right course of action when Reserved team members have shut off and isolated themselves.

As with all traits, overcoming struggles means some stretching, even to the point of discomfort. The Reserved individual can be coached to understand that when the amount they are contributing to the group and the amount of interaction with others feels uncomfortable to them, it is probably just about right. They may feel like they are talking too much but in all likelihood, their input is valued, appreciated and welcomed.

IDEAL WORK ENVIRONMENT

Working alone for extended periods in a quiet environment with time and space to think is ideal for the Reserved person. Typically tasks involving data, analysis, procedures, and details are more appealing to them than assignments that require a great deal of interaction with people.

Managing Reserved individuals includes some degree of guarding them from too much people-interaction. When you see schedules getting too full of meetings, remember they need their off-line time to process. Let them focus on projects and remember their need for closure. Don't drop by their office spontaneously and interrupt them with chit chat. Instead, set an appointment or call them and ask them if they have five minutes to talk before you arrive at their door. When you do this you will find them more receptive and ready for the conversation because a five minute (or more) warning or booking of an appointment offers them a chance to reach a stopping point in their work, so they can better engage with you.

Instead of expecting an immediate response, allow them time to reflect and process before answering. Invite them to participate in discussions by asking questions and affirming to them that you are genuinely interested in receiving their input. Trust is built over time with a Reserved person, and it will become easier and easier to engage them as the level of trust grows.

"Who is your Sandpaper Person?" is a question we ask during team sessions. That is, who is a person most different than you that just seems to rub you the wrong way? Reserved and Engaging individuals often name each other as their most irritating rub because the differences on the opposite ends of this factor play out on display for all to see. While the Reserved person may often think the Engaging person talks too much, the Engaging person may view the Reserved person as too uptight and closed minded, or even disengaged. But, the truth is we need both sorts of people on our teams, and they can work very well together if they learn to lean on each other's Strengths and adjust to each other's Struggles.

Factor 2 - Interaction

Reserved	Mid-Range	Engaging

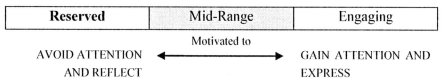

| AVOID ATTENTION AND REFLECT | Motivated to | GAIN ATTENTION AND EXPRESS |

If you have not taken Path4 online, consider the graphic above. Based on the information you have just read, do you believe you would score on the left-side, or Reserved side, of this trait? If so, mark an X on the graphic by Reserved. Or, if you possess a blend of the talents from both sides, mark an X in the Mid-Range section for this trait to show that you have Strengths and Struggles from both sides of this factor.

If you would like to take RightPath Path4 and Path6 profiles online, see Page 205 for instructions or visit www.rightpath.com.

Coach's Notes:

If you are Reserved...

If you are working with or leading a person who is Reserved...

CHAPTER 10

PATH4 – FACTOR 3
CONFLICT & PACE
HARMONIOUS (RIGHT-SIDE)

Factor 3 – Conflict & Pace

Challenging	Mid-Range	Harmonious

▪ Value Logic		▪ **Value Feelings**
▪ Confront		▪ **Support**
▪ Like Change		▪ **Like Stability**
▪ Impatient		▪ **Patient**

The third factor measured in Path4 evaluates **Conflict and Pace**. This factor indicates a person's need for harmony and the pace at which they like to operate. On the left-side of the continuum is Challenging and on the right-side is Harmonious.

This factor also measures a person's balance between feelings and logic. In addition, it indicates preference with regard to pace, change and conflict. People whose scores fall on the right side – Harmonious – tend to be compassionate behaviorally and tend to be able to "read" and assess the feelings of others well. Those who score on the left side – Challenging – can detach from situations and rely on logic more than emotion when assessing circumstances or making decisions.

Both logic and emotion are important. As a society, we need the balance of both sides of this, and all other behavioral continuums. In this case, the Harmonious side tends to be loyal, promote harmony and avoid conflict. The opposite site – Challenging –tends to move quickly and decisively and they are more comfortable with conflict because they see it as a method to bring about change and progress.

Those falling on the left, logical side of this factor tend to like a quick pace and are action oriented. Those on the Harmonious side however, prefer a steady, stable pace and are not usually eager in the initial welcoming of a lot of change. The right side naturally wants to promote stability while the left-side can become restless if things stay the same for too long.

With that overview, let's look at the Harmonious right-side of the continuum, which reflects individuals whose scores are 56 or higher in this factor.

Factor 3 – Conflict & Pace

Challenging	Mid-Range	Harmonious
Questioning	←——————→	**Harmonious**
Impatient	←————————→	**Patient**
Critical	←——————————————→	**Lenient**

Individuals who fall on the right-side of the continuum are often described as harmonious, patient, kind, and they can even become lenient. They are people pleasers who tend to get along well with others. These individuals are very relational but not just for the sake of interaction or attention. Those who score on the Harmonious side of this factor have a need to support others as well as the desire to promote peace and harmony.

HARMONIOUS TRAIT

Strengths:	Struggles:
• Operates best in harmony	• May compromise too much
• Compassionate and warm	• May be slow to confront
• A good listener	• Can be naïve and too trusting
• Patient, willing to wait	• Often resists change
• Loyal and consistent	• Can become passive
• Likes stability, works at a steady pace	• May be complacent
• Favors feelings, shows empathy	• May not verbalize true feelings

Can you think of some examples of Harmonious individuals? Think of likeable, but not necessarily outgoing or engaging people you know.

HARMONIOUS STRENGTHS

With a natural ability to be nice, Harmonious people tend to be called **compassionate, understanding, and supportive.** They are not driven by control or the need for attention as some of the traits we have discussed thus far. Harmonious individuals are motivated by the need for harmony as their name suggests. They tend to possess an image of an ideal world where people just get along. This is a viewpoint often lost in today's fast paced, constantly changing environment, particularly with the speed of technology added to the mix.

With a natural desire and **ability to support** others these individuals care about making others look good. Remaining in the background is fine with most of this group, as they are happy working behind the scenes to help make things tick smoothly. Sometimes they may receive little attention or recognition for what they do but don't mistake their lack of being lured to the limelight as meaning they don't need affirmation and feedback. They do.

Building relationships is a great Strength and comes naturally for Harmonious individuals. You will often find them working in roles such

83

as teaching, counseling, coaching and therapy. Their natural knack for both **extending and building trust combined with their sense of loyalty** serves them well in such roles.

Harmonious people are in demand and have retention in the workplace. Why? Because they get along with people. They promote harmony. These individuals are adept at involving people and building consensus. Harmonious people are **peacemakers as well as tolerant, team players.** They do not initiate dissention or argue for the sake of arguing. And when faced with such things they tend to naturally gravitate towards smoothing out the situation and finding a peaceable solution. Trying to see things from the other point of view is part of how these people operate. They do not naturally tend to assume they are right.

Not always but in many cases, they place great value on family and friends and the time they spend with them. **Relationships are a priority** for these individuals, particularly close relationships. They are loyal and protective of the people who are closest to them.

Think of the "steady Eddie" personalities you have worked with in the past; they may have exhibited Harmonious traits. They are **persistent, dependable, and like to operate at a steady pace.** Harmonious individuals bring a sense of stability to a work environment because you know what to expect from them. They are great at working on projects that involve a long-term commitment, and they can work in one place for an extended period of time without complaint. Barring issues such as a family illness or an emergency, they are not likely to miss work unless it is for a very good reason.

As peaceful as Harmonious people can be, staying so calm may not be ideal all the time. Sometimes, conflict is necessary to bring about progress or change. Sometimes, being quiet and peaceful can keep an organization or team stuck in a rut. So, let's look at the Struggle side where Harmonious individuals can perhaps take this loyal, supportive side a little too far.

HARMONIOUS STRUGGLES

Self-worth can be an issue for Harmonious people as a byproduct of their concern and sensitivity for others. Being sensitive to others is natural for them, but sometimes with regard to themselves they can also be **sensitive, naïve, and may compromise too much**. Because they are agreeable by nature, managers sometimes do not realize that Harmonious individuals need feedback to affirm how they are doing. They also may become easily discouraged when they receive feedback that is negative or just constructive.

Even when trust is not warranted, the Harmonious may extend it to others. Because of their natural optimism, they only see and want to believe the best about people. These individuals need to be particularly diligent not to be fooled or naïve or get caught up in deception. Manipulative people and those seeking control can often spot Harmonious individuals a mile away. They are perfect targets for a manipulator's plans and schemes. Discernment is the key for helping the naturally trusting Harmonious person to avoid being duped or used. A healthy dose of doubt or at least skepticism can help to balance out their sensitivity and sympathy so that they do not end up with their trust being betrayed.

Compromising too much and a lack of boundary setting can also be troublesome for the Harmonious. Whether giving away too much of themselves or giving away too much of their power, Harmonious individuals can lose sight of what they hold in order to please other people. Setting healthy boundaries is a very important skill for people with this trait to learn and practice both at work and at home. In coaching people with the Harmonious trait, the most consistent area you have to work with is boundary setting, especially when they are in a leadership role.

The word "No," does not come easily to the Harmonious person. Often when they try to deny a request being made of them, they encounter great resistance because people are accustomed to hearing

"Yes," from them. They are accustomed to saying "Yes," as well. Having the courage to say "No," to demands being made of them can be a critical part in a Harmonious person's personal development. That simple two-letter word – No – is often the one thing that stands between them and being overwhelmed. It helps at times to remind Harmonious teammates that sometimes "No" is the most loyal, caring answer. In fact, effective boundary setting is the key for people with this trait to be successful in the workplace and in leadership roles. As they see that agendas adjust and projects continue to move despite the occasional negative response or healthy boundary they set, the Harmonious person will find just what they hunger for – continued peace and progress.

While Harmonious people are well aware of their feelings and those of others, they **may avoid vocalizing those true feelings because they naturally avoid conflict.** Being **slow to confront** is not surprising for these people who like peace and harmony. They don't like to rock the boat. But, they need to learn to confront when necessary and appropriate. Ignoring problems does not resolve them. So, even though it feels uncomfortable, it is essential to help Harmonious individuals learn how to confront others when necessary and to view conflict as productive and necessary at times despite the discomfort.

If Harmonious people are not coached or coaxed to confront at the right time, they will put it off. This delay is not usually a good thing because it can result in passive aggressive behavior. Entering into conflict with a cool head, at the right time, and with good counsel is wise. But, waiting until situations escalate and entering in with a hot head (due to a build up from delaying) is not a good idea. Thus, Harmonious people are often well served by being encouraged to speak up while it is uncomfortable rather than to wait until it is too late or until they have reached a point where they might overreact.

Speaking out with their ideas is critical for all team members, Harmonious or otherwise. Only with complete input from a team's full complement of talents, are the best solutions arrived at and implemented successfully. With their typical reputation for being considerate, prudent, and reasonable, Harmonious teammates need to be heard and should not hesitate to contribute to discussions or to express their ideas. They are an important part of what holds a well-balanced team together.

> ### *IDEAL WORK ENVIRONMENT*
> ----
> *Provided there is some sense of harmony and stability in their role and/or organization, Harmonious people can be successful in most any work field that is of interest to them. When their efforts are part of growth, development and success of the organization and of others, they will find a sense of satisfaction.*

When managing Harmonious individuals or leaders, remember they prefer a steady pace and they have a need for harmony and stability. They will not be eager when change is on the horizon, so be sure to pay attention to them when change is in the works. Providing logic behind the change, as well as training and time to adapt to the change will help them adjust as their environment shifts. If you are faster paced than the Harmonious person working for you, it is wise to slow the pace of your communication and speech to allow them to relax and hear you without being stressed by your pressing tempo.

Factor 3 – Conflict & Pace

Challenging	Mid-Range	Harmonious

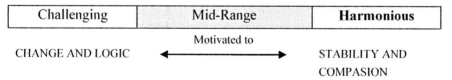

| CHANGE AND LOGIC | Motivated to ⟷ | STABILITY AND COMPASION |

If you have not taken Path4 online, consider the graphic above. Based on the information you have just read, do you believe you would score on the right-side, or Harmonious side, of this trait? If so, mark an

X on the graphic by Harmonious. If the information in this chapter didn't seem to fit you, your score is likely left-side (Challenging) or Mid-Range. The next chapter will discuss the Challenging Trait in more detail.

If you would like to take RightPath Path4 and Path6 profiles online, see Page 205 for instructions or visit www.rightpath.com.

Coach's Notes:

If you are Harmonious...

If you are working with or leading a person who is Harmonious...

CHAPTER 11

PATH4 – FACTOR 3
CONFLICT & PACE
CHALLENGING (LEFT-SIDE)

Factor 3–Conflict & Pace

Challenging	Mid-Range	Harmonious

- **Value Logic**
- **Confront**
- **Like Change**
- **Impatient**

- Value Feelings
- Support
- Like Stability
- Patient

The **Challenging** side of this factor consists of the "make something happen" type of people. Logical, quick thinkers, individuals in this group are decisive and never shy to tell you their opinion or solution. Physically, they move faster than their Harmonious counter parts and their minds move just as quickly. In meetings they are the ones pushing forward with the agenda and wanting to move on to the next decision or topic. Change is a constant for them; they love it and get restless with status quo.

Factor 3 – Conflict & Pace

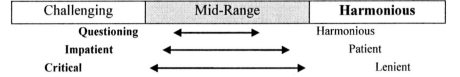

Challenging	Mid-Range	Harmonious

Questioning		Harmonious
Impatient		Patient
Critical		Lenient

CHALLENGING TRAIT

Strengths:

- Operates well in conflict
- Objective and cool
- Action-oriented
- Responds quickly
- Challenging, makes difficult calls
- Likes change, works at a fast pace
- Favors logic over feelings

Struggles:

- Can be combative
- May be abrupt
- Can be judgmental and critical
- Sometimes too impatient
- May tend towards hyperactivity
- Prone to discontent
- May appear coldhearted

The hallmark of a Challenging person is that he or she is not afraid to tell it like it is. They are easy to spot because they are opinionated.

CHALLENGING STRENGTHS

Challenging individuals are able to **detach themselves from emotion and situations to make difficult calls.** They are often called tough-minded and are logical in how they process information. Without emotion factoring heavily in their decision making, they can often make calls which are difficult and unpopular in the short-term, but are necessary in the long-term.

Making tough decisions is quicker and easier for Challenging people than for their Harmonious counter parts because they find it easier to be objective and consider just the facts at hand rather than the emotional elements or possible extenuating circumstances. While Harmonious individuals tend to not want to hurt anyone's feelings, the

Challenging individual thinks about the task at hand, the data collected, and is motivated to make a quick, decisive call.

Parents, leaders, managers, executives and individual contributors on teams are asked to make tough calls every day. Holding a staff member accountable for performance, deciding who will lose their jobs as a result of budget cuts or doling out some tough love are not easy things to do, but, they are easier for the Challenging group than for others because they are able to act decisively and then move on swiftly from that decision to the next step.

Conflict Is More Comfortable for Challenging People. That sounds a bit crazy for those who are more Harmonious by nature. It is true, however, that Challenging individuals see conflict as useful and often welcome it as a means of making progress and getting things done. They want to confront wrongs and with their thick skin they come out unscathed by the confrontation or conflict. They tend not to take things personally in the process of using conflict to reach a resolution or solution. Whether pointing out an order filled incorrectly at a restaurant or a CEO trying to get the corporate budget back on track, Challenging individuals will step up, speak up and seek to resolve the problem by confronting it head on.

You have probably seen the Challenging personality in action on many occasions. Picture a lively debate in a boardroom or courtroom. The Challenging enjoy it. Raised voices don't scare them. In the heat of conflict they are engaged and appear comfortable. Likely, not everyone around them is comfortable, particularly those who are Harmonious by nature, but they don't mind unsettling the conflict-averse people because there's a purpose to their passion.

Challenging people like things to be done yesterday. They are **action-oriented, fast paced, and are often change agents.** Placed in a slow moving environment, Challenging people become bored and restless. They prefer a fast paced environment and quick action. Challenging people email you and want an instant response. They move fast and like it best when others do too. If listening to a presentation, they prefer the bullet point version that moves quickly rather than the long, drawn out narrative.

Change excites the Challenging. If change is not afoot then they might just want to create it themselves! They are typically good at multitasking and can juggle a lot of responsibilities at once. Change, like conflict, is a tool that drives progress and they like progress and success. Change energizes them and is closely linked to their love of a challenge. Challenging individuals are motivated to rise to a challenge and come out on top.

The talents of a Challenging person make them well suited for environments that are unpredictable and in flux. Unexpected information, unpredictable occurrences and even crisis do not greatly surprise them. Rather' such occasions serve as opportunities that involve a challenge and inspire them to succeed.

CHALLENGING STRUGGLES

Detaching from emotion can be helpful in making hard decisions but the flip side of this coin is that Challenging individuals **can appear cold-hearted and insensitive to those around them**. Because they tell it like it is, and are quick to spout off their logic, those around them can see them as callous and uncaring. Challenging people can be insensitive to others and not even realize that they have hurt others' feelings. Because Challenging individuals almost always possess some degree of Directing behavior too, they can easily add insult to injury by acting or speaking without realizing how they are being received by other or how they are impacting others.

Particularly when focused on achieving results, Challenging people can drive the people who work for them very hard. Others' discomforts, needs, and feelings can be dismissed for the sake of progress if a Challenging person is unaware of the effects of their detached, insensitive behavior and high expectations. The danger of this struggle is that while it may bring the desired results in the short-term or medium-term as far as the organization or board of directors are concerned, it may undermine the team that was put under extreme pressure and duress to reach those results. People subjected to insensitive leadership may not want to hang around for the next assignment, particularly if there's a spot open somewhere else where they believe they will be more appreciated and better treated.

This doesn't always have to be the case though. Just because Challenging people don't naturally think about feelings, doesn't mean they cannot create learned behavior to work this consideration into how they operate. With coaching and guidance, even the most detached, Challenging leader can learn to appreciate that getting results at any cost is far inferior to getting results while valuing the people and relationships who are part of that success. Knowing they are not typically good at reading the mood of their staff, they can learn to ask those who are more discerning to help recognize when discouragement or frustration is surfacing around them. Often they will need help or coaching to see what they are overlooking.

A critical nature and judgmental spirit can often be attributed to Challenging individuals. Their ability to process information quickly, coupled with their focus on getting results, can lead them to readily identify Struggles in other people. Their intent is not to disparage the other person necessarily but more likely it's a desire to keep that Struggle from becoming a hindrance to the Results and success they are in pursuit of. What does this look like? The Challenging person may appear to have a low tolerance for a person or process. They may seem irritated and quick to confront others particularly when the pressure is on to perform. The Challenging individual usually justifies their impatience and criticism as "truth' which has become something they need to work around rather than something that needs understanding, accommodation, or help to better develop.

Tensions can run high particularly in a work group or home where there's a mix of Challenging and Harmonious individuals. The team or family can quickly divide into two camps and dissention can result just as fast if the critical Challenging camp has hurt the feelings of the Harmonious side. The answer again lies in understanding the opposing viewpoint to one's own. Because those on the Harmonious side have greater need for positive feedback and Challenging individuals can be critical or stingy in handing out "warm and fuzzy" feedback, tensions can rise. It helps for Challenging individuals to remember that when working with those opposite to them, dialing back the criticism and dialing up positive feedback is a good habit to keep things running smoothly.

It may help to remind Challenging individuals to consider instances where more positive feedback, although not natural for them to give, might have made a situation less tense and more productive. Some others they work with need that feedback to survive and thrive as part of a team. As with all learned behavior; it won't feel comfortable at first. Criticism comes much more naturally to the Challenging but once they see the results of meeting in the middle, the "stretch" out of their comfort zone is usually well worth the payoff.

Related to the Struggles discussed thus far, Challenging individuals are prone to **impatience, restlessness and can exhibit a constant need for change.** The same drive that keeps projects moving and gets things done can at times cause a Challenging person to want to move too fast. Impatience can be interpreted by those around the Challenging individuals as an indication that they are being egotistical and thinking that their agendas are more important than others on the team. When coupled with a need for control, Challenging individuals may *take* what they want – acting impulsively and impatiently – rather than going through proper procedures and channels. Others may see them as pushy or serving their own personal agenda above team or organizational goals and objectives.

In addition to impatience and impulsiveness, the desire for change can put stress on those in a Challenging person's sphere of influence. Harmonious people on the team don't adapt well to change, so if a Challenging person is too forceful with the subject of change, it can cause great stress as they anticipate additional work and problems they perceive to be associated with too much or unanticipated change. While Challenging people can survive and even thrive in chaos and a state of constant flux, operating in this manner often involves a high cost to a team if everyone is not comfortable with this mode of operation.

> ### *IDEAL WORK ENVIRONMENT*
>
> ----
>
> *Challenging people love to have a problem to solve or challenge to rise to. They enjoy a fast pace, love change and usually fare well in crises. Confrontation is a familiar tool in their tool box for getting things done so expect to feel that energy when working with them and provide them with plenty of challenges to help that energy be used productively.*

Being nice doesn't matter to the Challenging. **When managing this group of people there's no need to sidestep issues; they prefer frank, upfront dialog about the issues at hand.** Instead, tell it to them straight and fast while they are still listening. Offer them mobility in their role and be sure to keep the challenges coming, so they can put their energy to good use. They don't mind short-term projects and in fact, do well with them because they like to multi-task. Utilize them in a positive way to help drive change in a positive manner. Help them to tone down their critical nature. This is particularly important when dealing with their Harmonious counter parts who need more positive feedback and prefer information to be delivered in a slower fashion.

Whether it is learning to recognize and speed up to meet the high intensity needs of the Challenging side or learning to slow down and offer positive feedback to meet the needs of the Harmonious side, we all would do well to learn how to work well with our opposite team members in this third factor – Conflict and Pace. *This factor difference can create a lot of friction and tension.* Understanding our own wiring and that of those we work with in this factor will alleviate a great deal of strife in the work environment. Conflict can be used productively and change can be implemented much more effectively with a solid understanding of the right and left sides of this trait.

In coaching executives as well as in teambuilding, I saw this factor's differences surfacing intensely so often that it motivated lead us to create a curriculum called "Mastering Creative Conflict." The key word in this curriculum is "creative" because creativity is needed to bridge this factor for both the Harmonious and Challenging side. Helping individuals and teams to understand their natural, hard-wired, behaviorally rooted approach to conflict is powerful. Effectiveness of leaders, individuals, and teams is greatly improved as they learn how to utilize creative conflict as a positive force in the workplace.

Factor 3 – Conflict & Pace

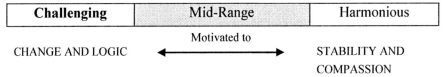

Challenging	Mid-Range	Harmonious

CHANGE AND LOGIC   Motivated to   STABILITY AND COMPASSION

If you have not taken Path4 online, consider the graphic above. Based on the information you have just read, do you believe you would score on the right-side, or Harmonious side, of this trait? If so, mark an X on the graphic by Harmonious. Or, if you possess a blend of the talents from both sides, mark an X in the Mid-Range section for this trait to show that you have Strengths and Struggles from both sides of this factor.

If you would like to take RightPath Path4 and Path6 profiles online, see Page 205 for instructions or visit www.rightpath.com.

Coach's Notes:

If you are Challenging…

If you are working with or leading a person who is Challenging…

Jerry W. Mabe

CHAPTER 12

PATH4 – FACTOR 4
ORDER
METHODICAL (RIGHT-SIDE)

Factor4– ORDER

Spontaneous	Mid-Range	Methodical

- Freedom
- Flexibility
- Impromptu
- Instinctive

- **Accuracy**
- **Scheduled**
- **Prepared**
- **Systematic**

The fourth and final factor – **Order** – in RightPath Path4 relates to how a person handles details, structure, organization and accuracy. The right-side of the factor is labeled Methodical where scores indicate someone has a natural tendency to work with details, likes to create structure, has an eye for precision and accuracy, and is motivated to be prepared, organized, and accurate. The left-side of this trait indicates a person's natural ability to operate well with freedom and flexibility, to estimate quickly and to operate in an instinctive and versatile manner.

Both the Methodical tendency to lean towards detail and structure as well as the Spontaneous tendency toward freedom and

99

flexibility play important parts in organizational effectiveness. This is a factor where mid-range is particularly noteworthy too as a person who exhibits a blend of the two sides employs talents from either side of the continuum. For certain roles/tasks, mid-range may be "just enough" methodical talent to be effective.

This Path4 factor is perhaps the one where people tend to see themselves most clearly, especially in our culture. This factor particularly plays out in a manner that is easy to see and draw comparisons and contrasts for most individuals. It is also a factor where, to be successful, one has to learn skills that help balance out natural "go to" behaviors.

Structure comes naturally to individuals who are Methodical. They typically like to be organized, well prepared and tend to have a good eye for accuracy and precision. These are characteristics demanded in some form or fashion by most jobs or roles and therefore, we all may *think* we have some of these abilities. The truth is, however, is that some people have to work hard on these elements while for others – the Methodical – they come very naturally and easily. Imagine your closet for a moment and you might just get a quick peek into your natural wiring on this factor. Is it color coordinated or divided up by items with everything hanging tidily? Is it like this all the time? Or, is one corner of your closet full of clutter? Are some items folded and others not, and are hanging items spaced haphazardly on the rail? Is it tidy sometimes but then gets messy with the hustle and bustle as days go by? If it's neat and tidy most of the time, you likely tend towards the Methodical side. Let's consider the Strengths and Struggles of this trait.

Factor 4– Order

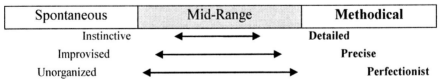

Spontaneous	Mid-Range	**Methodical**

Instinctive	←→	**Detailed**
Improvised	←——→	**Precise**
Unorganized	←———→	**Perfectionist**

METHODIAL TRAIT

<table>
<tr><th>Strengths:</th><th>Struggles:</th></tr>
<tr><td>• Organized and scheduled</td><td>• Tend to be inflexible</td></tr>
<tr><td>• Accurate with details</td><td>• May be too picky</td></tr>
<tr><td>• Establishes systems</td><td>• May over-rely on procedures/rules</td></tr>
<tr><td>• Prepared, rehearses carefully</td><td>• May over-prepare but lack confidence</td></tr>
<tr><td>• Analyzes before deciding</td><td>• Perfectionistic to avoid mistakes</td></tr>
<tr><td>• Conducts research to determine the facts</td><td>• May focus on details and miss the goal</td></tr>
<tr><td>• Responds diplomatically</td><td>• May be too formal, rigid</td></tr>
</table>

METHODICAL STRENGTHS

Laying on an operating table or handing over financial records compiled over your working lifetime, you would likely hope that the person whose hands your fate was in was **accurate, exhibited high attention to detail, was focused and thorough.** Methodical individuals at the extreme are sometimes driven even to the point of compulsion to get things right. The details matter far more than the time or energy it takes to get there. They do not like to make mistakes and definitely do not like to operate in a "trial and error" mode – **un**like their more Spontaneous counter parts. Methodical people are very uncomfortable with a "wing it" or "close enough" approach.

The higher a Methodical person's score, the more likely their bent for perfectionism extends into all areas of their work and life. Even when they have plenty of data and supporting evidence for making a decision they are on the lookout to see if there's more information, support, or reviews that might be found and factored in also. Research and investigation are a natural part of the process for Methodical people and often something they enjoy doing.

Generalizations or broad sweeping statements won't do for this group. They want to know the details and specifics. In most cases the jobs they are fulfilling require detail and they won't be afraid to ask for information, wait until they get it, and go through it with a fine tooth comb once received.

Methodical people are good at devising and following procedures. These individuals create structure around themselves. They are the people who actually *read* the instruction manual when they get a new appliance or gadget! Even more amazing, they are resolute to follow those instructions! Most enjoy a disciplined environment with rules to follow – it lets them know both what to expect and what is expected of them.

Many Methodical people are good at resisting distractions especially those who also exhibit a tendency towards being Reserved (left-side of Factor 2). They like to dot the i's and cross the t's as they ensure projects are completed properly and on time. Their drive to be thorough means they are typically good at persisting and reaching closure. In fact, they really prefer closure on one task or project before moving on to the next. This also means that if you step into their office to ask a question or tell them something, it is wise to let them know you are there. You should expect they will need a moment to finish what they are writing or doing before they turn their attention to you. It is better if you can avoid interrupting and plan your visit.

From the outside looking in, you may assume that Methodical people have a high need for Control and thereby assume they are also Directing (Factor 1). This may be the case but not necessarily. Methodical behaviors may or may not be linked to control. The distinction is that Methodical people have a need for control over information not necessarily a need for control in general. The need for control in general is more likely linked to the Directing trait. They are driven to get results and make sure outcomes are right but these drives in Methodical people are not due to the need to dominate or drive the boat. Rather they are focused on the goal, getting results, and the information and details required to do so. The drive is to achieve, not always to control. If a person is Directing and Methodical, then you are more likely to get synergetic control needs.

Disorganization causes distress for Methodical people. They prefer their workspace, projects and home to be **organized, scheduled, planned and prepared**. Open their desk drawer or closet and you'll find this to be true. Everything has a place and everything is in its place. A closet is likely color or item coordinated. Items in the desk drawer are segmented and tidy.

Heading into a meeting or presentation "unprepared" is a Methodical person's worst nightmare. They are planners who prefer to have their ducks in a row and all the details down pat beforehand. They try to anticipate the questions that will be asked and double check to be sure they have all their facts and figures straight. Research and planning are accounted for when projects are taken on. Meetings are recorded on the calendar and a timeline is plotted out even months in advance.

When traveling, the Methodical person likes to have an agenda and plan for the day, whether the purpose of the trip is business or pleasure. They check flight arrival and departure times as well as the Weather Channel and the Department of Transportation site for potential traffic delays. With a strong enough Methodical score, they may even set the radio program buttons in a rental car!

The ability to keep records, to take notes and to stay organized helps Methodical people in the work and academic realms. In an environment that is impersonal and which requires self-direction Methodical individuals tend to do well. So, whether it is a large class in a University setting or being a small player in a big corporate environment, provided they know what is expected of them and provided they have the resources and information they need – Methodical individuals will hunker down and get the work done.

Thinking of plans and procedures and taking the time at the outset to put them in place is a normal part of the process for system-oriented, Methodical people. The idea of starting a task or project without a well thought out plan is not an option. And, once they have a plan in place, they will be sure to use the time and effort in making that plan multiple times – if the plan and format fits other projects or assignments. Consider for instance, a presentation or project checklist and timeline. Any repetitive tasks will drive the Methodical person to develop systems in dealing with them. A key to the Methodical Factor is that these individuals use systems to create structure in any repetitive tasks.

Information on its own possesses no power. It is a matter of how that information is analyzed, assessed, and implemented that makes it useful. Methodical people know this. They are the ones who are **analytical, good at conducting research, and have a natural inclination toward understanding facts and data.** If you profiled the people who deal with creating research data at the CDC (Center for Disease Control) for instance, you would probably find most of them to be very Methodical. Sometimes analyzing data requires taking it apart and reassembling it. The same may be true when a Methodical person is trying to figure out how a piece of equipment might work; they study it, look at how it is made and even disassemble and reassemble it to figure out how it ticks.

Keeping their possessions in order matters to the Methodical group of people. They can also be **territorial** regarding that same stuff that they so carefully look after. They tend to be **disciplined and neat** as evidenced by our look into their closets earlier. While they may be generous at heart and happy to loan you something that belongs to them, they won't hand the item over without careful instruction on how to use and care for it. You will likely sense a little nervousness over whether it will be returned to them in the same condition it was when they lent it – especially if they think you are Spontaneous.

The manifestation of a Methodical individual's need for order will appear across many aspects of their life. While a not-so-Methodical person may pay attention to details with things they particularly care about, the truly Methodical person will exhibit these traits across virtually all areas of their daily life. He or she will straighten crooked pictures on the wall and notice if things around the house or office are in their place or not. In the kitchen you will likely find immaculately organized cupboards and refrigerator if they are the one who shops and likes to cook at home. Automatically, without a conscious thought, they put the groceries into the pantry with all labels facing forward and have some sort of system for how to stack those goods on the shelves whether it is by food type, alphabetically or by size. A key to the Methodical trait is that these individuals must be able to find things quickly when they need to use them. At work, Methodical individuals likely have a particular way that they like to organize their files or label their file folders. In fact, they tend to feel unsettled if they are not kept this way. Their desk may be piled with papers but those piles are organized in some fashion that they can quickly explain to you if they are asked.

METHODICAL STRUGGLES

Struggles are more often a result of strengths over-done than they are areas of a person's non-strengths. This truth is easy to see with the Methodical trait. Methodical individuals can **hold unrealistic standards (for self and others), strive for perfectionism and be too picky.** They may strive for perfect results past the point of diminishing returns. From writing an essay for school to compiling the most comprehensive data for a corporate report – at some point the collection needs can become beyond what is necessary.

Methodical people are hard on themselves. They often fail to realize that not everyone holds such high standards as they do, or that others do not all have their same high attention to detail. The fine details they are sure other people notice in their work is seldom as closely scrutinized as they imagine. The key for Methodical individuals is to find balance between their striving for personal and task perfection and the realization that perfection is an unattainable goal in most, if not all, instances.

Schedules and processes are helpful, but they can also be limiting – particularly in a fast-moving, quick-changing environment. For Methodical individuals their adherence to a schedule or their systems may cause them to be **rigid, over-rely on procedures and lack flexibility.** This has impact on dealing with change. Boundaries, plans, rules, and procedures are helpful until you come into a situation that requires thinking on the fly and a quick response. These individuals may be incredibly prepared, but they often suffer from fading confidence when they are placed in unpredictable or unfamiliar situations. They may have a tendency to rely solely on the preparation itself rather than their underlying knowledge, passion and abilities. Adding to their preparation a balance of confidence and flexibility is the perfect solution. A peer may help them role-play possible scenarios or questions to help build their confidence and remind them to trust themselves not just their procedures and processes.

Decision making that involves much attention to detail can often lead to paralysis by analysis for Methodical people. They may prepare the ammunition, load the gun, and aim over and over again but never fire. Their desire to hit the bull's eye dead center, the first time, may prevent them from ever pulling the trigger. Fact-finding and data collection can become the unintended objective rather than finding a solution based on sufficient data collected. Fear of taking risks can compound this tendency for some individuals.

Time is just one measure in a Methodical person's life. They like to keep schedules, plan and project. They also need to learn that sometimes timeliness of implementation is the bigger success factor than perfect implementation. That's a tough call for a highly Methodical person to make. For instance, taking a product to market quickly with 95% of the kinks worked out may mean success. On the other hand, if the Methodical team members insist on ironing out the last few kinks which would delay the launch and result in a marketplace flop, it's likely that the product will miss its opportune launch time and a competitor steals your thunder. That is to say, a good solution to a timely challenge may beat a perfect solution that is executed too late. Methodical individuals need to realize when preparation is sufficient and it is time to move. Often their more flexible or dominant (impatient) counterparts can help them learn to gauge when preparations are sufficient.

> ## IDEAL WORK ENVIRONMENT
> ---
> *Methodical people operate best in work situations that are process-oriented, structured, orderly, and systematic. They thrive where accuracy and details are important to success and are valued accordingly.*

Appreciate and encourage their systematic approach and attention to detail when **leading Methodical people.** More than attention to detail, they are typically committed to the details and to their accuracy. Respect their need for organization and planning by not coming to them in crisis mode, where possible. Instead, sit down and spell out the details of situations or needs and allow them time to process rather than expect an immediate response from them. Especially in public settings, try not to put them on the spot with unexpected questions. Rather, let them know ahead of time if you plan to call on them for input or expertise in public situations. Or, intentionally or get their answer last in a group meeting allowing them time to process before answering. Where possible, allow them time to search out the facts, research, analyze details and thoroughly prepare their response.

Factor 4 – Order

Spontaneous	Mid-Range	Methodical

Motivated to

FREEDOM AND FLEXIBILITY ←————————————→ ACCURACY AND STRUCTURE

If you have not taken Path4 online, consider the graphic above. Based on the information you have just read, do you believe you would score on the right-side, or Methodical side, of this trait? If so, mark an X on the graphic by Methodical. If the information in this chapter didn't seem to fit you, your score is likely left-side (Spontaneous) or Mid-Range. The next chapter will discuss the Spontaneous Trait in more detail.

If you would like to take RightPath Path4 and Path6 profiles online, see Page 205 for instructions or visit www.rightpath.com.

Coach's Notes:

If you are Methodical...

If you are working with or leading a person who is Methodical...

CHAPTER 13

PATH4 – FACTOR 4
ORDER
SPONTANEOUS (LEFT-SIDE)

Factor4– ORDER

Spontaneous	Mid-Range	Methodical

- **Freedom**
- **Flexibility**
- **Impromptu**
- **Instinctive**

- Accuracy
- Scheduled
- Prepared
- Systematic

The word **Spontaneous** is used to describe the naturally motivated behaviors of the group who score to the left-side on Factor 4 in Path4. These people are instinctive and tend to work as generalists. Too much required attention to detail will cause them to get frustrated and restless. They much prefer the 50,000 foot view and they are excellent at "going with the flow." They like to move and work quickly, unrestricted by details and rules.

Factor4– Order

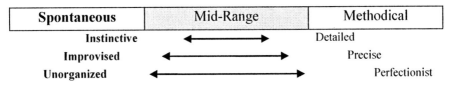

Spontaneous	Mid-Range	Methodical
Instinctive		Detailed
Improvised		Precise
Unorganized		Perfectionist

Spontaneous people often like to be on the move and may also come across as gregarious particularly if they are also Engaging. While the group of Methodical people we just discussed like to analyze things, this opposite group prefers synthesis to analysis. Spontaneous people like to move from idea to idea and task to task and at a fast, changing pace. They process best "on the fly" by taking in information as it comes to them through experience, conversations and mobility. Often, but not always, Spontaneous people tend to be visual learners as well as communicators. Give them a whiteboard and markers, get out of the way, and you'll see what I mean!

SPONTANEOUS TRAIT

Strengths:	**Struggles:**
▪ Flexible and versatile	▪ Not naturally organized
▪ Works with broad concepts	▪ May "wing it" too much
▪ Improvises, operates without procedures	▪ May ignore rules
▪ Instinctive, operates spontaneously	▪ May be under-prepared but over-confident
▪ Make on the spot decisions	▪ May be impulsive
▪ Gives a reasonable estimate	▪ May overlook important details
▪ Responds candidly	▪ Too informal when formality is needed

SPONTANEOUS STRENGTHS

The quick-to-start Spontaneous group often appraises situations and information on-the-spot. Assessing the big picture is a Strength for Spontaneous individuals. In social settings or situations where there is much noise and information, they are quick to take it all in and get a feel for the dynamics of the room, the task at hand and the players involved. Their outward focus tends to allow them to quickly scan the environment.

Ask a Spontaneous person about a previous situation or a particular piece of information, and they may close their eyes as if they are trying to picture where they last saw that information or what the scene was like that is being inquired about. With their tendency to reply quickly, don't expect them to give you an answer that is exact in every minute detail, that is in a sequence or written on paper. They prefer approximations or estimations and will usually include something about the bigger picture or the general context of the situation. Their gut response or off-the-cuff reply is often very close to reality.

Their random access memory skills make Spontaneous individuals well suited to dynamic tasks or fields where on the spot assessments are required – like crisis management, customer service, sales and other areas where individuals must read the situation quickly and react accordingly. They are able to rapidly cover a great deal of ground in their thinking. In fact, they don't like to stay focused on one area of thought for too long or they find themselves becoming bored and unfocused. Mobility and variety are paramount in their work world.

Spontaneous individuals are experts at last minute preparation and typically do their best work under pressure. The challenge and excitement of the pressure cooker makes them to shine. When preparing a speech their notes are loosely organized, not highly structured, and the delivery is never identical, word-for-word, two times in a row. Each time it is delivered in a new and improved manner. If not, they find it boring and "stale". Plus, it is no fun if you don't change it!

Deadlines force Spontaneous individuals to get into gear and work quickly in the moment. Last minute preparation is their signature style and actually, if forced to prepare too far in advance, they lose their edge because the information is not fresh in their mind and experience.

Versatility and flexibility are two key indicators of a Spontaneous person's trait playing out. Seeing things in general terms and thinking of the big picture allow Spontaneous individuals to improvise easily. Without knowing all the details, they are often able to grasp general concepts. They see the horizon and landscape not just the elements within three feet of them.

Energy and excitement flow from these individuals. Preparation is an outline to them, not a detailed plan which has to be executed through every single detail. When the winds change, they can adjust their plan and shift accordingly. When opportunities arise, they are ready to take hold of them. This trait helps in situations where the details are out of one's control such as in live entertainment, on the team playing field, and in fast-paced industries, or careers like technology or sales.

They are sometimes considered **unconventional** because they often respond very **candidly and openly.** Because Spontaneous people don't fret over the small details, they are often quick to respond with opinions and thoughts – an action which gives off an air of confidence. Because they often say what they think, sometimes they don't even take themselves too seriously. They are more aware than anyone that they can change their assessment, opinion, or course of action in a heartbeat – so it's best not to get too attached to what that is in any given moment.

Spontaneous individuals often "fly by the seat" of their pants and seem to perform best when they have to pull things together at the last minute. They can push limits, challenge rules and defy procedures, because they lean heavily on their instincts rather than established protocol or regulations to guide them. Trusting their gut can cause them to break rules, at times, but a confident leader will also take responsibility for his or her Spontaneity and its outcome.

SPONTANEOUS STRUGGLES

Multi-tasking can also look like working randomly and too quickly for the Spontaneous. They can become **disorganized, lack preparation and rely too heavily on instinct.** Organization is not natural for these individuals and they have to work hard at it. Keeping up with papers and schedules can seem bothersome to them. Leaving home or the office, they often leave something behind – a pen left on the desk of a coworker or glasses left on the kitchen counter and misplaced car keys are common occurrences for these people. In a real rush, it can become a whole trail of "left behinds" in their wake to exit.

It is not that they don't have good intentions of being organized and orderly. At times, they may try to create order in their workspace to help them focus more clearly. The challenge is that as they get busy and their mind and body are set in motion, the organizational facets are the first to fly out the window. Prone to distraction, they may begin one task and jump to three others before even realizing they haven't completed the first. Because they are often very visual, finding an organizational system or filing method that works for them is critical – for some it may be alphabetical, for others by project, others with good memory for dates may prefer to organize things sequentially in their filing cabinet or email inbox. Successful Spontaneous people will say they have had to inevitably learn to create structure. Some have developed such strong "learned" structure that teammates often think they are Methodical. They are quick to tell others how much they have to work at that structure, though!

The good news is that organization is easier than ever with modern technology and it's an area where strong learned behaviors can help bridge the gap for Spontaneous individuals. However, the same technology that makes organization easier, has also given us much more information to handle and that information often arrives at the speed of light. The most valuable advice for Spontaneous individuals is to get some training in the area of organization, find a system that works for them, and keep working at it. With Spontaneous leaders, we coach them to find Methodical support to delegate the details, using their differences well.

Preparing in advance and highly detailed preparation are challenging for this group. If forced to prepare too early, they can lose their edge in making presentations because they work best when ideas and information are fresh in their memory banks. The thought of detailed preparation can be daunting and they tend to procrastinate, preferring the "rush" and adrenalin of the last minute scramble.

Their optimism can help bolster their team and build enthusiasm but it can also cause Spontaneous individuals to Struggle when it comes to giving a realistic estimate of how much work or time it is going to take to complete a project. Although they are naturally good at estimates, preference for moving quickly can cause them at times to be overly optimistic, particularly under pressure or deadline. While they do their best work in crisis mode, lack of advance preparation can undermine their whirlwind of activity.

In order to avoid incomplete assignments, missed deadlines and half-finished tasks, Spontaneous people need accountability and a realistic person to act as a sounding board for their high flying and 'on the fly' plans. A good accountability person or coach will help lead the Spontaneous individual to self-coaching as well by encouraging them to think of what the expectations are of them, what the finished product will look like and to anticipate any potential pitfalls.

IDEAL WORK ENVIRONMENT

At work, Spontaneous people perform best in environments that require flexibility, allow them to bank on their natural intuition and require on-the-spot responses. Broad concepts and impromptu settings are comfortable to them.
Most Spontaneous people will prefer mobility in the workplace to being confined to a chair or desk all day. Details are part of most any job. However, breaking structured assignments into bite size pieces will help these individuals remain focused through to completion.

As their teammate or leadership coach, it's important to **manage the Spontaneous** in a manner where they know that your goal is to help them reach their highest potential, so give them maximum opportunities with their talents. Accountability is necessary for them although they may not always like being reminded to stay on task. Thankfully, they are usually a light-hearted group and so a little humor and tangible incentives can help keep them on track and seem less burdensome. They thrive in the heat of the moment and learn best by experiencing that pressure and performing through it. So, if they are reasonably prepared, set them free and they won't disappoint.

In this Factor called Order, we see our friends, family and coworkers. We all know individuals who are meticulous with details and plan everything well in advance. We also know people who are chronically late and whom we might always tell that a meeting or party starts thirty to sixty minutes before the real start time with the hope that they might actually be on time for the event. Both sides of this factor have merits and value. It is one factor where most of us have to learn some of the skills from the opposite side of the spectrum. Spontaneous people synthesize dynamics of situations while Methodical individuals analyze data and information. Both are necessary and seldom is success reached without an element of both sides of this coin.

Spontaneous individuals need to learn to prepare, meet deadlines and adhere to procedures albeit more loosely than their Methodical counter parts. Methodical individuals need to learn to go with the flow at times or learn to pull the trigger realizing they may never have complete information before making decisions. Both sides need to find a balance of structure and flexibility that allows for overall team and organizational success. Learning and using the assets offered by those on the other side of the continuum will allow both sides to leverage the other's expertise and affirm the value of each

Factor 4– Order

Spontaneous	Mid-Range	Methodical
FREEDOM AND FLEXIBILITY	Motivated to ←——————————→	ACCURACY AND STRUCTURE

If you have not taken Path4 online, consider the graphic on the prior page. Based on the information you have just read, do you believe you would score on the left-side, or Spontaneous, of this trait? If so, you have probably already flipped to the next page of the book! But in case you haven't, mark an X on the graphic by Spontaneous. Or, if you possess a blend of the talents from both sides, mark an X in the Mid-Range section for this trait to show that you have Strengths and Struggles from both sides of this factor.

If you would like to take RightPath Path4 and Path6 profiles online, see Page 205 for instructions or visit www.rightpath.com.

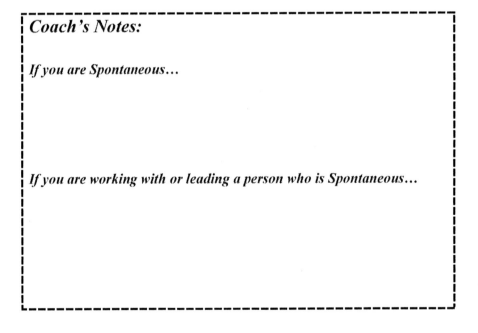

Coach's Notes:

If you are Spontaneous...

If you are working with or leading a person who is Spontaneous...

CHAPTER 14

FOUR FACTORS WORKING TOGETHER, THE POWER OF THE BLENDED PROFILE

Understanding the individual factors as measured in the Path4 behavioral traits is akin to having four puzzle pieces. How these pieces fit together will look different for various individuals. A person who is Directing and Methodical is going to "fit together" differently than one who is Directing and Spontaneous. And so, considering all four of the Path4 factors collectively, RightPath has compiled sixteen Blended Profiles that fit the manner in which behavioral traits typically present themselves.

If you have completed Path4 online, your report will indicate the Blended Profile that most closely fits you under the graph on page two of the report. The circles on the graph represent the Blended Profile and the squares represent your scores. Blended profiles are statistically measured and assigned by the validated algorithms used in RightPath's web-based assessments. The profile assigned is based on the closest fit to your scores, particularly in your most prominent traits.

For illustration purposes, we will use our case study person named Richard Results. The graph on the following page indicates that Richard Results is classified as a Driver (Blended Profile). His scores track closely to the blended profile but are even more extreme (higher on the right-hand side, and lower on the left-hand side) than the Driver Blended Profile markers for three of the four factors shown on the graph.

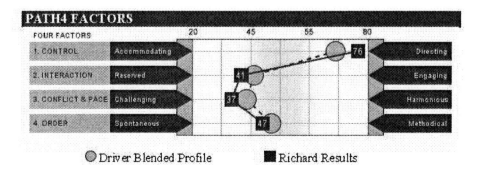

Note how the shape of Richard Results' scores as shown by the square markers is similar to the shape made by the circle markers for the Driver Blended Profile. The behaviors are similar in location and intensity although Richard is even more Directing than the typical Driver profile.

Clearly grasping how your own traits work together in this blended fashion helps you to more completely understand yourself from a behavioral perspective. The same is true for the people on your team and those whom you might lead.

The image on the following page gives an overview of the sixteen possible blended profiles that are assigned according to the RightPath Path4 profile. Then, each Blended Profile is described individually including coaching tips for how to work with and lead individuals who fit each of the sixteen particular Blended Profiles. Remember: The Blended Profile names serve as a learning and retention tool – they are not intended to label or "pigeon hole" individuals.

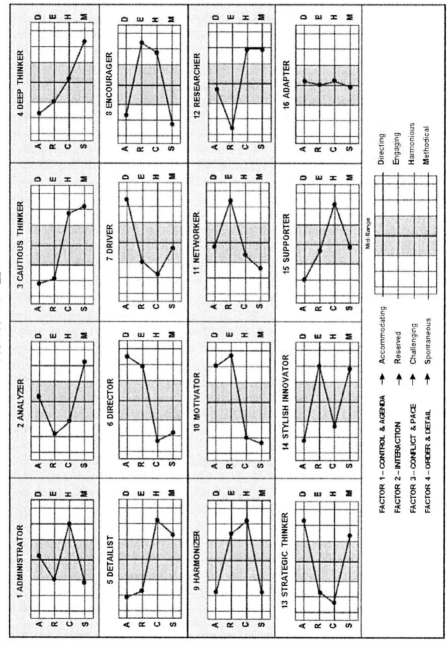

1 - ADMINISTRATOR

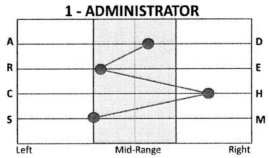

UNIQUE BLEND: Factor 3 is on the Right-side and Factor 1 is Mid-Range or to the Right-side.

ADMINISTRATORS combine the ability to get along with people with the determination to reach goals and accomplish tasks. This blend of personality strengths makes them well suited for situations where consistency, reliability, and persistence are important.

STRENGTHS: They are persistent, goal-oriented people who promote team effort among employees in order to complete tasks. They also make good leaders by blending patience with firmness.

STRUGGLES: They may not say what they really think. Sometimes they appear to agree but really don't and then backpedal. Can be stubborn, inflexible to new alternatives, and slow to change. Can be sensitive and take things personally.

IF YOU ARE AN ADMINISTRATOR, AS A LEADER CONSIDER: Your patience is one of your greatest assets in leadership. However, holding others accountable and dealing with confrontation may be your least favorite aspects as you lead. Building consensus will allow you to get results and reach goals, provided you do not shy away from making the hard calls. This is where letting your firmness rise to the occasion will see you through to deal with tough issues.

LEADING OR WORKING WITH ADMINISTRATORS: Give them a challenge and basic guidelines, and then let them do it their way. Recognize their achievements. Respect their privacy and earn their friendship over time.

2 - ANALYZER

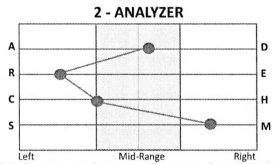

UNIQUE BLEND: Factor 4 is on the Right-side and is greater than Factor 1 which is Mid-Range or on the Right-side.

ANALYZERS are very task-oriented and seek to balance the desire to obtain results with the desire for perfection. They are very competitive individuals who excel at evaluating the work setting and initiating changes to produce better results.

STRENGTHS: They tend to be analytical, logical, direct, and confident. They like new challenges. They excel at seeing the larger vision, creating efficient methods and procedures, and listening carefully for the facts.

STRUGGLES: They may lack sensitivity to the feelings or efforts of coworkers. They may also come across as critical, curt and impatient.

IF YOU ARE AN ANALYZER AS A LEADER CONSIDER: Your natural goal-orientation and propensity to get results are hallmarks of your success as a leader. Seeking to avoid paralysis by analysis will help you lead without getting bogged down in too many details. The window of opportunity can close so get feedback to see if you are moving out appropriately. As a leader, it's important that you build trust with those you lead in order to make delegation easier for your detail-oriented self.

LEADING OR WORKING WITH ANALYZERS: Deal with specifics and facts and avoid emotional expressions. Honor their need for structure and give them time to analyze and prepare. Give them the whole scope up front to allow their analysis strengths to be best applied. Be clear on your expectations, desired outcomes, and deadlines up front – define what success looks like and they will strive to achieve it.

3 – CAUTIOUS THINKER

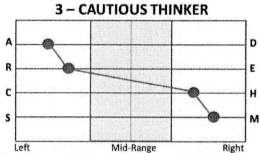

UNIQUE BLEND: Factor 4 is greater than Factor 3 and both are on the Right-side. Factor 1 is on the Left-side.

CAUTIOUS THINKERS take great care to be accurate and thorough in their work, preferring to contribute by being precise, systematic, and using careful reasoning.

STRENGTHS: They are organized, logical, analytical, thorough and accurate in their efforts.

STRUGGLES: Sometimes they are too picky and may overanalyze and delay making decisions. They can be pessimistic about outcomes and critical of others who don't meet their standards.

IF YOU ARE A CAUTIOUS THINKER, AS A LEADER CONSIDER: Your collaborative attitude, patience, and attention to detail make you a likeable leader. In leadership, your greatest challenge may come from your tendency towards being reserved. Speak up both to and for the team that you lead, and you'll see their trust in you, as their leader, grow even stronger. Remember to speak up and out. It is also wise to engage others who are less risk averse to help you see the big picture and know when to stop analyzing and pick up the pace in making decisions.

LEADING OR WORKING WITH CAUTIOUS THINKERS: Give them time to process information and time to "get it right." Encourage them to share their ideas. Protect them from pressure and minimize risks. Give feedback if you see them overanalyzing or getting paralyzed. Remind them they don't have to have *all* the answers to move forward.

4 – DEEP THINKER

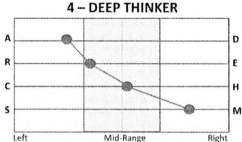

UNIQUE BLEND: Factor 4 is the only one on the Right-side and Factor 1 is on the Left-side.

DEEP THINKERS are analytical, logical and philosophical in their search for meaning, truth and purpose in their work. They are particularly adept at drawing incisive conclusions from data and research.

STRENGTHS: They are logical, organized, conscientious, thorough, analytical and prepared. They are focused workers who strive for high standards, precision and integrity in their work.

STRUGGLES: They may come across as distant or cold in relationships. They often underestimate themselves. They may not express disagreement and choose to go along with a decision; then later resent it.

IF YOU ARE A DEEP THINKER, AS A LEADER CONSIDER: The people you work with admire your ability to cut to the chase and explain things clearly – so lead confidently! Use this to your advantage when setting goals for your team by helping everyone understand and gain buy-in to their part of reaching the goal. Be sure to speak up so your input is not lost if you are working with more vocal counterparts.

LEADING OR WORKING WITH A DEEP THINKER: Encourage their input. Give them logic, details and facts. Avoid surprises. Give them time to prepare and time to process changes. Offer support by acknowledging what they do well as this will boost their lower self-estimation. If you don't get a clear read where they stand on a topic, then ask. They may hesitate to disagree or express divergent opinions, especially early on in evaluation.

5 - DETAILIST

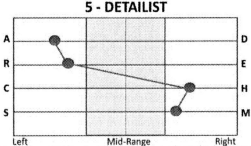

UNIQUE BLEND: Factor 3 is greater than Factor 4 and both are on the Right-side. Factor 1 is on the Left-side.

DETAILISTS are very attentive to details that are often overlooked by others. As a result, they are typically very organized, self-disciplined, and recognized at work for being both dependable and accurate.

STRENGTHS: They are typically conscientious, cooperative, dependable, organized, thorough, analytical, cautious, patient, steady, understanding and harmonious.

STRUGGLES: They may be too cautious, unassertive, and may put off making tough decisions. They may spend too much time on details and not keep pace on key projects.

IF YOU ARE A DETAILIST, AS A LEADER CONSIDER: You are a loyal leader, dependable, and on top of all the details. Your team appreciates your great patience and cooperative attitude. Keenly aware of deadlines and goals set for you and your team, you like to deliver and do so well. Beware of your tendency to avoid the hard conversations with your staff or desire to continue gathering information when the time has arrived to stop processing and make a decision. Don't let your detailed strength inhibit your ability to lead effectively and take action.

LEADING OR WORKING WITH DETAILISTS: Draw them into the discussion and encourage their input. Slow down the pace and be an active listener. Avoid intense or harsh expression, or showing impatience while they process, and minimize conflict. Provide feedback if you see them getting "stuck" in their quest to get *all* the info and preparation.

6 - DIRECTOR

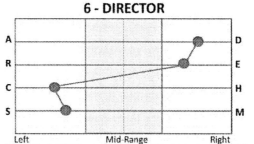

Left   Mid-Range   Right
UNIQUE BLEND: Factor 1 is greater than Factor 2 and both are on the Right-side.

DIRECTORS usually have a unique blend of confidence, initiative and people skills. They typically are able to see the larger vision and use their excellent communication skills to motivate others toward reaching it.

STRENGTHS: They are typically outgoing, bold, optimistic, fun-loving, competitive, confident and assertive. They motivate others to accomplish tasks. They excel by having the freedom to define organizational goals and by influencing others to reach those goals.

STRUGGLES: They are impatient and usually poor listeners. They may talk too much and can be judgmental and harsh. They tend to have strong egos and unrealistic optimism, often struggling to finish what they start.

IF YOU ARE A DIRECTOR, AS A LEADER CONSIDER: Quick, bold, and decisive are words that people would use to describe you as a leader. You engage others to get the job done and cast vision well, but you may become impatient if progress is not at the pace you desire it to be. Keep yourself keenly aware of deadlines and avoid underestimating work required for completing a project. Focus and finish what you start – on time! Last minute adrenaline can be habit forming!

LEADING OR WORKING WITH DIRECTORS: Speak directly, challenge them, and expect them to challenge your ideas. Offer options and then help them prioritize to get closure on their many projects. Remind them of deadlines and help them stay focused on tasks to reach completion. Challenge them to finish projects fully and not let the details (and boredom) at the end of a project stop them from finishing strong.

7 - DRIVER

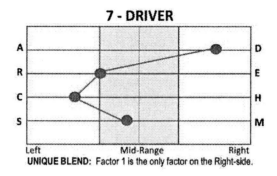

UNIQUE BLEND: Factor 1 is the only factor on the Right-side.

DRIVERS are people who create activity and set the pace within an organization. Due to their desire to lead, they quickly take charge of work settings by defining goals and delegating tasks. They are not afraid to take risks or strong action in order to achieve the desired results.

STRENGTHS: They are bold, direct, confident, competitive, often pioneering, assertive, frank, independent, responsive to new challenges, and capable of creating a direction focused on results.

STRUGGLES: They tend to be poor listeners, opinionated, blunt and distrustful of others. Highly independent, they have difficulty accepting and carrying out someone else's ideas.

IF YOU ARE A DRIVER, AS A LEADER CONSIDER: Leading is natural for you. You are quick to take charge and confident in your abilities to reach the goals set for you and your organization. It may be hard for you to accept input particularly when it is contrary to your own ideas or beliefs or when you are wanting to move faster in making decisions. Remember to listen without interrupting! Others can have great ideas and, at times, can save you from making a wrong turn.

LEADING OR WORKING WITH DRIVERS: Keep communications short and to the point. Give them bullets and options. Let them reach their own conclusions. Help them remember details and commitments by putting them in writing and getting their commitment and sign-off up front. Help them to get ownership in ideas and projects. They work best if they feel that what they are working on was their idea!

8 - ENCOURAGER

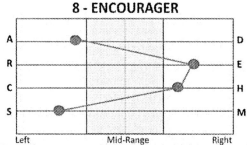

UNIQUE BLEND: Factor 2 is greater than Factor 3 and both are on the Right-side.

ENCOURAGERS are naturally relational and seek to be responsive to the needs of others. They make great listeners, responding to challenges of helping others in practical ways, including solving personal problems.

STRENGTHS: They are typically energetic, friendly, encouraging, patient, understanding, loyal, steady, dependable, and are very versatile in the workplace.

STRUGGLES: They have a strong need to be liked. May delay making decisions, waiting for a consensus of opinion. May have trouble saying "no," and may neglect work objectives trying to meet the needs of others.

IF YOU ARE AN ENCOURAGER, AS A LEADER CONSIDER: You are a well-liked leader, seen as patient, steady, and dependable. You build strong relationships in order to get the results you desire and you are always willing to hear the input your team has to offer. Making the hard call can be a challenge for you so it is important to consider the cost/impact of delaying difficult calls or conversations when you are tempted to avoid conflict. Don't let your desire to be liked get in the way of giving honest, candid feedback when a strong word is needed.

LEADING OR WORKING WITH ENCOURAGERS: Remember their need for fun and excitement. Keep them involved with people and give them opportunities to be in the limelight. Help them set boundaries and learn to say "No." Give them feedback if you see them trying too hard to please others and not giving constructive feedback when it is needed by others.

9 - HARMONIZER

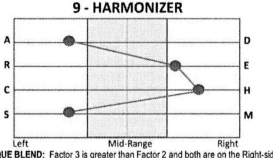

UNIQUE BLEND: Factor 3 is greater than Factor 2 and both are on the Right-side.

HARMONIZERS excel at promoting harmony and cooperation within an organization. Their natural inclination is to help and support others to carry out a task and to build teamwork in the process.

STRENGTHS: They foster a cooperative team effort in their work by seeking ways to help, carrying out directives, completing tasks, negotiating, and delivering encouragement in practical, tangible ways. They relate well to people and excel at conveying care and compassion. They are also very versatile at work.

STRUGGLES: Harmonizers usually have difficulty setting boundaries. They may avoid taking action or speaking up if conflict is anticipated. Harmonizers also may lack confidence and not express their good ideas.

IF YOU ARE A HARMONIZER, AS A LEADER CONSIDER: Inclusive leadership is your style as you create a work environment that is functional, productive, and encouraging. If you are leading individuals who are more dominant than you, setting clear boundaries and expectations will be critical to maintaining your authority and achieving success with your team. Remember if you can't reach consensus you have to step up to the situation and take the lead.

LEADING OR WORKING WITH HARMONIZERS: Lower the intensity and avoid harsh, direct talk. Acknowledge feelings (yours and theirs) and seek their input. Acknowledge their contributions to others. Hold them accountable when the time comes to rise to the occasion, give critical feedback, and deal with issues – especially people issues.

10 - MOTIVATOR

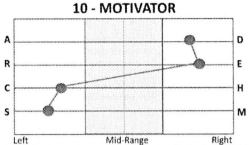

UNIQUE BLEND: Factor 2 is greater than Factor 1 and both are on the Right-side.

MOTIVATORS excel at blending their high energy and enthusiasm with the desire to achieve goals and results. Their superior communication skills enable them to motivate effectively an audience or workforce and mobilize it to action.

STRENGTHS: Typically they are passionate, highly interactive people who love to achieve, influence, and relate with others, especially large groups. They thrive on variety, change, new challenges, and the chance to convince others of their views. They optimistically point to the future.

STRUGGLES: They may dominate the conversation and not notice that others are not interested. They tend to exaggerate. They are sometimes overly optimistic and impulsive. May get emotional under pressure.

IF YOU ARE A MOTIVATOR, AS A LEADER CONSIDER: You bring energy to a room and to your team. Multi-tasking is your specialty along with interacting with people. Your optimistic preference for the big-picture and variety rather than the finer details may cause you a challenge particularly when you and your team have specific deliverables or deadlines looming. Be aware that you need to work to read others' needs and avoid being overly self-focused.

LEADING OR WORKING WITH MOTIVATORS: Help them channel their energy and enthusiasm. Realize that some elevated levels of emotion may accompany that great energy and drive. Encourage opportunities for high-profile exposure. Help them focus their talent for influencing others. Assist them with EQ (Emotional Intelligence) when they are not reading others' needs or put their interests above team goals.

129

11 - NETWORKER

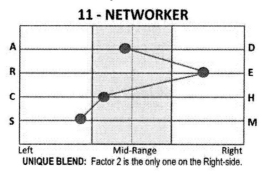

UNIQUE BLEND: Factor 2 is the only one on the Right-side.

NETWORKERS enjoy new people, new situations, and new environments. They use their people skills to build relationships and interact with an ever-widening circle of contacts. They enjoy using their verbal skills and wit to be very engaging and persuasive.

STRENGTHS: They are normally strong communicators. They are outgoing, engaging, lively, optimistic, gregarious, persuasive, fun-loving, enthusiastic and inspiring.

STRUGGLES: They may talk too much, be too emotional and too optimistic and may struggle with organization and details. They tend to over-commit and have difficulty finishing a task.

IF YOU ARE A NETWORKER, AS A LEADER CONSIDER: You know a lot of people – those you lead and those inside and outside the workplace too. You are an engaging leader and approach the task at hand with an optimistic viewpoint which can sometimes cause you to underestimate the time it will take for you or your team to complete various tasks. Switching gears is easy for you and you use your circles of influence to help you and your team get the job done. Realize that structure and organization are your struggles and learn to create structure that works for you. Use tools and support to keep yourself organized.

LEADING OR WORKING WITH NETWORKERS: Include them in the group. Get their opinions and ideas. Accept their need for things to be fun. Help them transfer their talk to completed action. Recognize they struggle with deadlines and organization so help them create structure. Provide tools and resources that help them create the needed structure.

12 - RESEARCHER

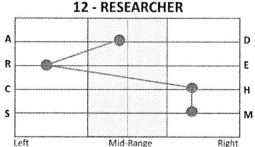

UNIQUE BLEND: Factor 3 and 4 are on the Right-side. Factor 2 is on the Left-side, and Factor 1 is Mid-Range or Right-side.

RESEARCHERS are very task-oriented people who like to see the job completed efficiently, accurately, and on time. Capable of resisting distractions, they stick to the assignment until it is completed.

STRENGTHS: They are typically very productive people in the workplace. They blend their desire to achieve goals with the desire for accuracy. They are motivated to become competent experts in their fields.

STRUGGLES: They can come across as cold, blunt, and rigid perfectionists. Highly task-oriented and independent, they typically dislike socializing and may be judgmental of those who operate through relationships.

IF YOU ARE A RESEARCHER, AS A LEADER CONSIDER: Knowledge and information are power for you. Your ability to pay attention to detail and to envision the end result allow you to set clear vision for your team. The challenge for you, however, will be that you are quiet. You would rather share vision with your team in written form, rather than verbal form, which may make you seem aloof to your team. Schedule time to force yourself to connect personally to others, especially those on your team.

LEADING OR WORKING WITH RESEARCHERS: They prefer written over verbal communications. Keep conversations brief and to the point. Respect their expertise and build your credibility over time to develop the relationship. Hold them accountable for learning to be more relational and working to build solid relationships.

13 – STRATEGIC THINKER

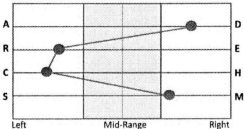

UNIQUE BLEND: Factor 1 is greater than or equal to Factor 4 and both are on the Right-side.

STRATEGIC THINKERS excel by blending their strong drive to achieve goals with a desire for precision, accuracy and quality. As a result, they are equipped to lead in situations where achieving results in a challenging environment is a priority.

STRENGTHS: They are goal-oriented, precise, analytical, assertive, confident and prepared. They insist on high standards. They have a good eye for detail and push to get the job done right.

STRUGGLES: They can be picky, pushy and controlling to get results. Quick thinkers, they are often impatient, critical and poor listeners. They have difficulty accepting others' input and hold stubbornly to their ideas.

IF YOU ARE A STRATEGIC THINKER, AS A LEADER CONSIDER: You want to lead and are very comfortable holding the reins of leadership. You are a confident and well-prepared leader who insists on quality work, on time, and on budget. With attention to detail and the need for control, you may struggle with trusting those around you to perform the task at hand until they have proven their ability to do the job and do it right. Slow your pace to take time to listen to others' input and ideas. It can become too easy to stick with your idea at the risk of missing a better one from someone else's input.

LEADING OR WORKING WITH STRATEGIC THINKERS: Keep it short and on point. Give options rather than initially contradicting them or telling them what to do. Feed them facts so they can reach their own conclusion. Expect them to confront you with questions. Show your rationale, stand your ground, and use logic to help them see another view.

14 – STYLISH INNOVATOR

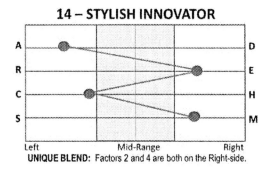

UNIQUE BLEND: Factors 2 and 4 are both on the Right-side.

STYLISH INNOVATORS are motivated to create lasting and favorable impressions by using precise, technical information and skills that inform, train, influence or persuade people. Making this impression involves developing an area of expertise and access to groups of people.

STRENGTHS: They excel at promoting new ideas, stirring up high energy and enthusiasm of new projects, and drawing on their wide base of knowledge to successfully promote their agendas.

STRUGGLES: May lack focus, take on too much, then try to do it all perfectly leading to overwhelm. Can be emotional and critical under stress.

IF YOU ARE A STYLISH INNOVATOR, AS A LEADER CONSIDER: Stylish innovators have a unique ability to promote their agenda and engage others to get the job done. You are a relational leader with attention to detail. This unique blend allows you to focus on details and results while simultaneously building relationships and engaging others in the task at hand. Recognize that you may "connect the dots" faster than others and check to make sure your expectations are realistic. Be careful not to show impatience when others don't "get it" as quickly as you do.

LEADING OR WORKING WITH STYLISH INNOVATORS: Include them. Be sure to get their input before making decisions. Look for "limelight" opportunities so they can express their creative ideas and gain public recognition. Help them realize the gift they have in being oriented to both relationships and results. Assist them in understanding that they are a quick study and point out (and hold them accountable) for not becoming impatient when others don't catch on as quickly.

15 - SUPPORTER

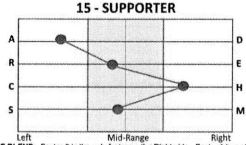

Left   Mid-Range   Right
UNIQUE BLEND: Factor 3 is the only factor on the Right-side. Factor 1 is on the Left-side.

SUPPORTERS naturally thrive when given the opportunity to help, encourage or cooperate with others. They are loyal friends and employees and gain fulfillment by helping make others successful.

STRENGTHS: They typically are excellent team players, due to their desire to cooperate, help others, and listen. They desire to be patient, loyal, and steady and to support the efforts of those in charge.

STRUGGLES: They may delay tough decisions or actions to avoid conflict and have difficulty in saying "No" or setting boundaries for others. They typically resist changes and are slow to initiate.

IF YOU ARE A SUPPORTER, AS A LEADER CONSIDER: As a leader, you always consider the impact on your team. Your desire for a cohesive, collaborative team compels you to ensure team members feel included and valued. Staff appreciate your patience but strong personalities will certainly challenge your ability to set and uphold boundaries. While boundary-setting is uncomfortable, it is necessary for success. Use your gift for building consensus then rise to the occasion and "toughen up" (set boundaries) to confront others when consensus is ignored.

LEADING OR WORKING WITH SUPPORTERS: Remember their need for stability and harmony. Lower the intensity level and soften the tone of communications. Encourage their input and then actively listen. Acknowledge the value of their support. Hold them accountable for standing their ground and giving others critical feedback when it is needed. Appeal to their sense of helping others and remind them also that confronting others may be the best help, in some cases.

16 - ADAPTER

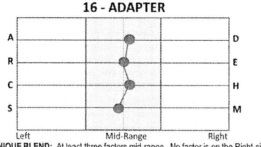

UNIQUE BLEND: At least three factors mid-range. No factor is on the Right-side.

ADAPTERS typically have the ability to adapt to the needs of their environment. They are very versatile and can be very good team players.

STRENGTHS: They have a natural ability to evaluate the situation and adjust their style to work well with others. They usually have a strong desire to please, and so they are quick to devote their skills wherever they are needed to get the job done.

STRUGGLES: They may be indecisive when there are conflicting opinions, and may have difficulty in setting boundaries for others and themself. They may get overwhelmed and not tell anyone.

IF YOU ARE AN ADAPTER, AS A LEADER CONSIDER: Your tempered leadership style allows you to see both sides of the behavioral coin for the people you lead, work with and work for. Based on the situation, you can take the driver's seat or sit back and let others working for you rise to the occasion. One of your greatest strengths may be your ability to offer a tempered response and the flexibility that makes you such a versatile leader. Because you can approach things from various angles and do not have a high need for control, others may not be able to predict how you will act or react particularly in highly charged situations. Communicate your opinions and force yourself to take a position.

LEADING OR WORKING WITH ADAPTERS: Recognize their contributions. Encourage them to share their opinions and ideas. Help them prioritize and develop systems and work relationships that reduce stress. Hold them accountable for expressing their opinions openly, communicating clearly, and taking a solid stand on issues.

Jerry W. Mabe

CHAPTER 15

TEAM DYNAMICS,
LEARNING TO LEAD/INFLUENCE A TEAM

With what you have just read and learned about the four Path4 Behavioral factors and their corresponding Strengths and Struggles, you now possess the foundational behavioral keys to unlock your team's potential and collective Strengths as well as identify its likely Struggles and common pitfalls. This knowledge is paramount for leading people uniquely, and for leading teams. We constantly hear from leaders who have used Path4 and Path6 for themselves that they are amazed at how much what they have learned about the traits also applies to teams. The next logical step that follows personal leadership development is for a leader to apply his or her learning to leading teams.

Before we talk about the overarching elements of team success, unity, and trust in the next chapter, let's see what we can uncover about a team based solely on their behavioral talent "fingerprint." When we facilitate team sessions, what we call the team matrix (displayed on next page) is shared and participants are often surprised how much they can learn to predict dynamics and interaction in teams, based on behavioral tendencies and traits. I think you will be surprised at the new knowledge you now possess too.

Just like individuals, all teams have Strengths and Struggles. A team's collective Strengths and Struggles come from the traits of its members and the balance and interaction that those members display across the behavioral traits. Have a look at the team matrix below and on the next page. Follow the prompts to note what you can learn and predict from its "behavioral footprint."

RightPATH® 4 Profile Team Matrix
Sample Team A

Accommodating	Mid-Range	Directing
	Andy Administrator	Al Adventurous
		Dan Daring
		Donna Director
		Danny Driver
		Mindy Motivator

Reserved	Mid-Range	Engaging
	Andy Administrator	Al Adventurous
	Dan Daring	Donna Director
	Danny Driver	Mindy Motivator

Challenging	Mid-Range	Harmonious
Al Adventurous	Dan Daring	Andy Administrator
Donna Director	Mindy Motivator	
Danny Driver		

Spontaneous	Mid-Range	Methodical
Andy Administrator	Danny Driver	
Al Adventurous		
Dan Daring		
Donna Director		
Mindy Motivator		

Review Team Matrix on the previous page.

What are this team's likely Strengths?

What are this team's likely Struggles?

How is Andy Administrator different than his teammates?

What is Andy Administrator likely to impact on his team?

What would happen if you added a person who is Accommodating, Reserved, and Methodical to the team?

Now, compare your notes on the prior page to our observations below.

Team Strengths: This is a team of people with drive to accomplish results and succeed.   Five of the six team members are Directing.   They are also all people-oriented and good at engaging an audience and others. The team is likely fast paced, talkative and flexible.

Team Struggles: There may be a battle of wills going on here as five of the six team members naturally will want to be in control and driving the team.   Their meetings are probably loud, talkative and rarely follow a set agenda or they jump around, if one is set.   It is a group of highly opinionated people which may leave us to wonder if they are unified in goal and mission.   Following rules, attention to detail, organization and meeting deadlines are probably a collective Struggle for the team.

Andy Administrator is the only Harmonious one on this team. He will be uncomfortable when conflict erupts on the team, preferring a slower paced, more harmonious environment.   At times he is likely unsettled in meetings with his teammates as they jostle for control and speak bluntly with one another.   If you pay attention, you may notice he is checking his watch to see how much longer until the meeting is done. If he does speak up, it will likely be with a view to sort things out, to move to consensus, or to diffuse the situation rather than to become an integral part of the heated discussion.

Adding a Harmonious, Reserved, Methodical person to the team would mean that person is a fish out of water on virtually all traits when compared to the current teammates.   If this person was a support person for the other team members, it would be very important for him or her to understand how the Directing teammates operate.   The existing team mates would need to understand that he or she needs time to process information and will not jump into discussions at meetings.   When they want an opinion from their Reserved team mate they will need to ask and preferably give that person time to process the request and prepare their reply.

In reality, this is actually a Sales Executive Team I have worked with. The executives on the report need to take initiative and operate independently out in the field day after day. So, their Directing nature helps them to "go get 'em" as well as initiate contact with clients and lead field sales reps that report to them. They need to be able to communicate with clients, make on the spot decisions and adjust their actions or pitch based on the circumstances they encounter and "read."

As with many Sales Teams, especially those that are not highly technical, attention to detail is not one of the team's strengths. Support people and processes can be employed to help fill the gap and keep the details in order as these individuals go do what they do best – sell, drive revenue, and add new clients. Because they are a decisive, quick moving group, they need the freedom to use their ability to make on-the-spot decisions in order to get results. But that also means sometimes someone will need to do the follow-up behind them and take care of the fine details of fulfilling the orders sold and the commitments they have made.

Adding balance to a team like this is accomplished through definition of roles, management and leadership style and structure of support staff for this group. Looking at the Team Matrix on page 136, there are gaps in the traits of Reserved and Methodical. It is helpful to understand that these gaps do not necessarily need to be filled to create balance. Unless it is a technical or highly specialized sale, hiring a Reserved sales rep would likely not work out well since the team works well at present with individuals who are mid-range or right-side on the Engaging trait. The same caution is true for the Methodical trait. Just because there's an absence in this area, you do not have to fill the gap. People wired that way might get so caught up in the details that they will fail to move and close the sale.

In most cases, teams of people in similar roles are going to show similarities in behavioral traits. You'd never expect to find a group of neurosurgeons for example, who were very Spontaneous and who lacked attention to detail. In other roles however, you may see a greater diversity in behavioral talents and traits. For instance, some corporate trainers are Directing and Engaging, enjoying both the independent and relational parts of their role. Other corporate trainers may be more Accommodating and Harmonious, driven to succeed by a desire to share information and help people learn rather than by their own need for attention.

So, how do we know what behavioral talents fit particular jobs or roles? Path4 gives us a great overview of behavior and teams like this. We call Path4 an x-ray which is great for quick diagnosis and serves as our introductory learning tool. Path6 we call our MRI because it adds much greater insight through the use of subfactors that provide a deeper look not just at behavior but also at the motivations behind those behaviors. Thus, Path6 is better for evaluating specific behavioral and talent fits in an organization. To do this we use Path6 to profile top performers and create benchmarks (or success profiles) that have proven success in selection and reducing turnover. Refer to Chapters 16-21 for more detail on Path6 and its use.

Teaming for Success

It is a very rare situation where a person works or lives entirely on their own – independent of the support, help, leadership, counsel, and cooperation of others. The corporate and workplace trend has been moving more and more to the work team concept for decades now. As humans we need each other and hopefully, after reading through the prior chapters on behavioral talents you now understand a little more about why that is the case. Each individual brings unique talents to the table and only through working together can those talents be multiplied as a team. Teammates working effectively together can accomplish far more than those same individuals would accomplish individually on their own.

Why is that? It's simple really. A well-structured team allows a leader to leverage talents so that each individual contributor is working where his or her best talents are engaged and employed. Whether "raising" a barn, launching a new product into the marketplace or running a state of the art hospital, there can be strength and talent in numbers – and in differences (behavioral inclusion/diversity).

The protection, support, division of labor and talent offered in a team setting has benefits even for the person who considers himself or herself a loner. Complementation is a benefit of teaming and working with others. The root word "complete" says it all and defines a well led and self-aware team! Although a Reserved person may prefer interacting with a few people to interacting with a crowd, he or she still benefits from collaboration and community as do their teammates from the Reserved person's input.

In this chapter we will explore some key foundational concepts of teaming which build on the behavioral (talent) information we discussed thus far. Team diversity/inclusion, unity and trust are core elements to employ when building strong, effective teams.

Capitalizing on differences and using an inclusion/diversity of talents to build strong teams. A team that consists of teammates who are all behaviorally identical can be a recipe for disaster. For example, a team of all Directing personalities can look much like a boat with too many captains fighting over who will be at the helm. A team overloaded with Spontaneous talents may rarely if ever meet a deadline – at least not on time! An overly Challenging team may move too quickly and neglect the people-related aspects of their business and there would likely be a struggle with too much conflict developing on an ongoing basis. Teams need diversity/inclusion in talent and make-up but unity in mission.

The *key* to building effective and diverse teams is to use the power of differences to **unite rather than divide**. This can only be done when people are self-aware, understand, accept, appreciate and even capitalize on the differences between themselves and their teammates. It serves leaders and teammates well to understand their own behavioral talents and also develop an appreciation for the talents of those who are different too.

What Is True Diversity? Inclusion!

Many people think of diversity solely in terms of age, race, gender, and national origin. Removing prejudices and biases that undermine fairness and respect in the workplace is important along those lines and many others. Divisive situations have made this a hot topic in American leadership in the past number of decades. From the divisions between management and labor unions to divisions due to age, race, gender, or ethnicity, companies have had to find ways to remind individuals of common goals. Organizations also have to deal with differences that can exist due to geographic cultural differences, experiential differences, gender issues and the generation gap.

The truth however is that, although those elements may be easy to identify about individuals at a glance, we at RightPath believe they are not the best angle from which to help people understand the value of diversity, build unity, and achieve inclusion. While it is possible that two engineers may experience conflict in the workplace because one is male and the other female; they now are much more likely to be at odds over things like deciding how much research is enough to act on, or over the two individuals wanting to be in control of the same project. When we facilitate diversity/inclusion sessions for corporations, participants most often discover that they have much more in common with people whose behavioral talents are similar to theirs regardless of their race, gender or color. These differences can become powerful unifying factors.

Whether differences are more behavioral as I just suggested or related to lifestyle, age, gender or race, the more we can help leaders to see diversity/inclusion as an issue of valuing all people, regardless of their differences, the more cooperative and cohesive our teams will be – and effective too!

By looking at the core behavioral factors of Path4, we realized that objectivity is critical when looking at ourselves and others. Because we tend to view others through the tint of our own behavioral glasses, learning to understand those who are different than us is the first step in understanding that difference doesn't mean "of lesser value." In fact, the differences can bring value and unity to our teams.

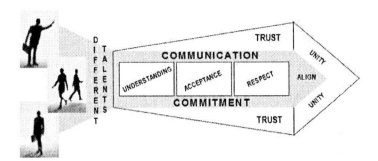

Teams need unity in mission, commitment, corporate values, loyalty, policy, discipline and opportunity. These core elements need to be understood and embraced by all team members. Each member should be able to express their team's mission, values and core elements of unity at any given point in time.

But teams *also* need diversity in talents, Strengths, Struggles, motivations, ambitions, ideas, interests, needs, styles and worldviews. From the foundation of a unified mission, diverse talents, abilities and ideas will allow for the individuals on the team to successfully employ their individual abilities. A strong team celebrates and appreciates the contributions of its members as it works together towards the common good or goal. Without such appreciation, disagreement and confusion can arise causing a breakdown in team trust, commitment and unity.

Diversity/inclusion can be described as difference, variety, innovation, variance, change, and flavor. Diversity is an infusion of different talents and ideas. Diversity is a much broader perspective than just equal opportunity. Inclusion – true diversity – occurs when those differences are understood, accepted, respected, and used to complement (complete)! Consider the piece parts of the diagram above.

Uniting different talents into successful teams leads to team success. You can see in the diagram of the team model that communication and commitment are the "rails" on which an effective team runs, leading to success.

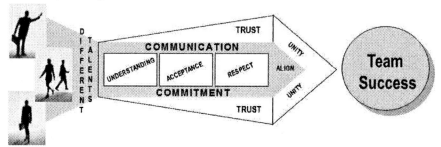

Communication ensures that team members are informed and on the same page. This communication needs to take place in all directions; from manager to staff, staff to managers and among peers. It also includes the necessary interaction with others in an organization that are *not* on the team.

Commitment to team goals, corporate objectives and to teammates goes hand in hand with communicating with those on the team. Once the mission is understood and embraced, the commitment to the greater good propels the team forward. Strong teams are committed to the team's overall objectives and to the subsets of goals that each team member strives for as part of those overall goals. Furthermore, effective teams are committed to the individuals who make up the team even if they don't work together day in and day out. Team members need to know and understand each other in order to be committed to and appreciate each other. This understanding includes different Strengths and Struggles.

Understanding differences allows teammates to appreciate the talents each team member brings to the table. Teammates who learn to value different Strengths and accommodate different Struggles are not only more productive but also more supportive of one another. Seeing individuals' Struggles as part of the package that comes with Strengths allows us to appreciate differences.

Accepting differences broadens team members' horizons as they realize that not everyone has to think, act, or work like they do. Learning to listen to others' "off-the-wall" ideas might just bring your team and your company the next million dollar idea!

Respecting others' differences allows us to celebrate both the person and their talents. It is right to respect others simply because that's the "right" thing to do, but beyond that, showing that respect allows others to achieve their full potential. When people are respected they feel encouraged, empowered, and valued. In turn, they are motivated to perform well and return the respect to those that they work with and for as well.

Individuals make up teams. And, individuals have individual points of view. Each member on a team that seeks to perform at its best must realize that they, as individuals, are a part of the whole. The team will need to adapt and align their behavior, where necessary to facilitate the relationships within the team. When a Challenging person on the team adjusts her tone to speak to her Harmonious team member, information is communicated more effectively and delivered with more respect. Further, when an Engaging manager wants the input of his most Reserved staff member he is wise to give her time to process and then seek her input later in the day or even the following day, rather than requiring an immediate response. Such alignments make a team more functional and successful. As team members learn and understand how they are wired and how their teammates are wired they adjust better to those differences for the benefit of the team and its success.

When these things are done well, trust is built. Trust is developed as a byproduct! An environment based on trust is efficient because time is not wasted. Furthermore, motives are not questioned, positions need not be defended unnecessarily, and work gets done. This doesn't mean there won't ever be conflict – there will. But it allows a team to have Creative Conflict! It does ensure that team members know there are no hidden agendas or ill motives at play. Stress for the entire group is kept in check, satisfaction increases and work is more enjoyable when teammates trust each other. Without trust, a team's success is quickly compromised.

When trust is absent a team and its members become selfish and self-focused – not results-focused. In his book, *The Five Dysfunctions of a Team*, Patrick Lencioni calls this "artificial harmony." Individual ambitions can override the greater good. Controlling behavior tends to surface as do insecurity and insincerity. Distrust causes team members to be pulling in different directions rather than unified in purpose and motion. If this is happening on your team, there's good news. Trust can be rebuilt; it can be developed.

The key to building (or rebuilding) trust is removing self-focus. By focusing on others rather than self, team members can learn to communicate effectively, walk the talk, care about others, operate in a realm of transparency, and concentrate on a team agenda rather than private agendas. "Artificial harmony" can transition to real harmony. Teammates need to be consciously working on good relational skills including effective listening, seeking input for decisions, offering support to those who need it, and spending time to be sure that everyone is on the same page.

Each team member brings value. Differing talents in team members are necessary for overall success. The way to make the most of the talents at hand is to focus on others in the team. Develop and encourage one another in areas of talent. Seek out and become role models. Applaud successes and rally together when mistakes are made. And, mistakes will be made even on the best of teams. In fact, sometimes in recovering from mistakes, teams become even stronger for having weathered a storm successfully, together. Truly effective teams learn from mistakes and grow together, increasing trust. It is important for individuals to develop and for the team as a whole to continue to improve and develop also.

Coach's Notes:

What components of my team need work, based on the model diagram shown on pages 145-146.

Jerry W. Mabe

CHAPTER 16

PATH6
THE BEHAVIORAL MRI

RightPath's unique approach involves using two profiles that work *together* to provide strong internal validation with both a behavioral X-ray and MRI, much like the way medical professionals may use a physical X-ray and MRI. We have already explored the RightPath Path4, our "X-ray," which looks at the basics of behavioral talents. Four factors with two sides to each are easy to teach and understand. But, just as the MRI can show more detail than an x-ray, Path6, our "MRI," allows individuals to better see and predict the motivations and underlying elements of core behavioral factors. While we don't expect to turn you into a behavioral talent "doctor" in an instant, we want to give you as much knowledge as possible. We expect that the added Path6 insight of subfactors and adding two new behavioral factors will help you to understand behavior and talents better and more deeply. Thousands of clients say they are easy to use, and they love the depth of new understanding with the two profiles working together.

The factors of Path6 are strongly correlated but not identical to Path4. They are correlated, yet distinct. The profiles are similar while also unique. Their descriptions are similar but more detailed in Path6 because of the use of subfactors. This allows the two tools to internally validate each other and also add value by showing nuances and differences between the two. The forced choice nature of the Path6 tool also makes it stable over time and minimizes impact of situational considerations when individuals complete the profiles online. While you likely could estimate your behavioral marker for the four factors of Path4, it is unlikely you can as easily guess at your Path6 scoring areas because of the introduction of subfactors. If you have not done so and would like to take the Path4/6 profiles, refer to the login information on page 205 or visit our website at www.rightpath.com for information on how to purchase and complete the profiles.

It is important to look beyond just the Factor scores of Path6 and consider how the subfactors influence behavior as well. If the subfactors are closely clustered together for a factor then you can assume the individual will be true to the general description of its factor. The strongest of subfactor scores (farthest to the right or left from midpoint of 50) will tell you what elements of that factor you can expect to see most clearly played out with an individual. For instance, someone who is Dominant will have scores for the three subfactors: Assertive, Independent and Blunt, which work together to show you how the Dominance will display itself in their day to day interactions and actions.

Two New Factors

In Path6, a new fifth factor is added – **Adventurousness.** The elements comprising this factor are blended into the Directing (Factor 1) in Path4. Because Adventurousness plays out differently than pure Dominance and is so important in leadership we felt it was important to report its score on its own. Path6 allows us to measure it on its own. For example, someone may like a challenge and be daring without necessarily being Dominant.

In Path6, we also added a new sixth factor called **Innovation.** It is important to understand this is not a measure of "whether" a person can innovate, *but rather* a measure of **how** a person typically approaches innovation. RightPath believes all people are capable of innovating. However, we may do so differently. Some of us innovate through abstract thinking and unbridled creativity while others of us are more practical and experiential in how we come up with ideas and solutions. Both are innovative in the end but differ greatly in how we get there!

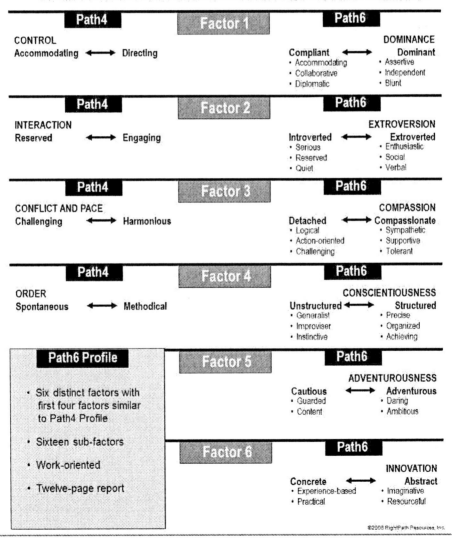

Profile Comparison

The first four factors of Path4 and Path6 are similar and the scores generally correlate for most people.

Path4	Factor 1	Path6
CONTROL		DOMINANCE
Accommodating ⟷ Directing		Compliant ⟷ Dominant
		• Accommodating • Assertive
		• Collaborative • Independent
		• Diplomatic • Blunt

Path4	Factor 2	Path6
INTERACTION		EXTROVERSION
Reserved ⟷ Engaging		Introverted ⟷ Extroverted
		• Serious • Enthusiastic
		• Reserved • Social
		• Quiet • Verbal

Path4	Factor 3	Path6
CONFLICT AND PACE		COMPASSION
Challenging ⟷ Harmonious		Detached ⟷ Compassionate
		• Logical • Sympathetic
		• Action-oriented • Supportive
		• Challenging • Tolerant

Path4	Factor 4	Path6
ORDER		CONSCIENTIOUSNESS
Spontaneous ⟷ Methodical		Unstructured ⟷ Structured
		• Generalist • Precise
		• Improviser • Organized
		• Instinctive • Achieving

Path6 Profile	Factor 5	Path6
• Six distinct factors with first four factors similar to Path4 Profile		ADVENTUROUSNESS
		Cautious ⟷ Adventurous
		• Guarded • Daring
		• Content • Ambitious

Path6 Profile	Factor 6	Path6
• Sixteen sub-factors		INNOVATION
• Work-oriented		Concrete ⟷ Abstract
• Twelve-page report		• Experience-based • Imaginative
		• Practical • Resourceful

©2006 RightPath Resources, Inc.

153

Jerry W. Mabe

CHAPTER 17

PATH6 – FACTOR 1
DOMINANCE

Factor1– Dominance

Compliant	Mid-Range	Dominant

▪ Indirect	▪ Direct
▪ Tactful	▪ Frank
▪ Non-confrontational	▪ Bold
▪ Cooperative	▪ Commanding
▪ Team Player	▪ Takes Charge

Dominance is measured in the first Factor of Path6. Dominance can be defined as the degree to which a person is commanding, exerting authority or influence. The left-side of this factor (Compliant) describes a person motivated by dealing diplomatically with people using relational talents to get things done. The right-side of this factor (Dominant) describes a person's motivation to assert him or herself, to operate independently and frankly in the drive to get results.

Like Path4, each side of the behavioral continuum has its relevant Strengths and Struggles. The Strengths for each side of the Dominant factor are listed on the next page. For Path6, we are not dedicating a page for each side of each factor. Instead, we are reviewing the

Strengths and Struggles of both sides of every factor in a "point – counter-point" manner. We then offer insights into the subfactors that comprise the overall factor score.

Compliant	Dominant
Strengths:	**Strengths:**
• Loyal – follows the set agenda	• Initiating, wants to set agenda
• Process-oriented	• Results-oriented
• Speaks tactfully	• Speaks directly
• Cooperative – promotes stability	• Competitive, likes challenges
• Moves cautiously into new areas	• Moves boldly with confidence
• Focused – likes to do one thing at a time	• Prefers multiple projects
• Sees the practical for here and now	• Sees strategic/future potential

In general, **Compliant** individuals are typically more agreeable when working with others, enjoy the joint efforts of working with others, and are careful when choosing words and making comments. The **subfactors** used to comprise this score are Accommodating, Collaborative and Diplomatic.

Factor 1 - Dominance

Compliant	Accommodating	Mid-Range		Assertive	Dominant
	Collaborative			Independent	
	Diplomatic			Blunt	

Accommodating: relaxed, supportive

Collaborative: consensus-builder, team-oriented

Diplomatic: tactful

Assertive: dominant, forceful, influencing, take-charge

Independent: self-reliant, individualistic

Blunt: candid, direct, frank

Individuals with a strong score in the Accommodating subfactor are supportive of established agendas. The Collaborative subfactor measures their preference to operate with others. The Diplomatic score indicates their tact in dealing with others and tendency to think carefully before speaking.

Dominant individuals' scores are broken down into the

subfactors of Assertive, Independent and Blunt. The way Dominant behavior displays itself looks different for the person who is highly Assertive compared to one who is less Assertive and more Independent. The Assertive subfactor shows a person's initiative to take charge, shape their environment, influence others and be a visionary out in the lead. Independent individuals are self-reliant, confident in their own abilities and prefer to operate alone as much as possible. Those that are Blunt, tell it like it is in the most direct manner possible and often are not as careful with their word choice as others. They may catch themselves retracting or "explaining" later.

Compliant	Dominant
Struggles:	**Struggles:**
▪ Can be unassertive, timid	▪ Opinionated, discounts others
▪ May tend toward being passive	▪ May be controlling
▪ May be hesitant to speak out	▪ Typically not good listeners
▪ May avoid taking charge	▪ Prefers to avoid routine/details
▪ Tends to underestimate self	▪ Can be self-centered, egotistical
▪ May agree, then regret and resent it	▪ Underestimates work needed to achieve goals
▪ Sees the practical for here and now	▪ May over-commit what others can do

Both sides of the factor and their corresponding subfactors have Struggles as well as Strengths. On the Compliant side, a person may underestimate themselves (Accommodating), hesitate in making decisions if they need too much input from other people (Collaborative), and their tendency towards diplomacy may cause them to withhold their true opinions even when asked directly (Diplomatic).

For the Dominant people, their Struggles lie with being too forceful or opinionated (Assertive), reluctant to collaborate with others (Independent) or too harsh when speaking to others (Blunt).

Now, let's look at a real example to help apply these subfactors to a person. We have learned from our train-the-trainer program that it is easier to understand the factors when you see a "live" example. We will look at our case study person, Richard Results.

Take a look at Richard Results Path6 Factor 1, Dominant Score and his accompanying subfactors.

DOMINANCE

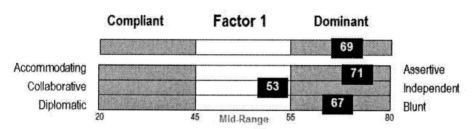

Richard's Factor 1(Dominance) score is clearly on the Dominant side of the first Factor with a score of 69. Further analzying that score are the accompanying subfactors of Assertive (71), Independent (53) and Blunt (67). The factor score is strong so he clearly comes across as a Dominant person. He is highly Assertive. In fact, that is his strongest subfactor. His Independence moderates to 53 which is in the mid-range indicating that he likes to work with others better than one might expect for someone so Dominant. And, based on his blunt score of 67, you know his natural tendency will be to "tell it like it is." Does this better explain how Path6 helps to identify how a person can clearly be highly Dominant but in ways very different and unique than others who are equally Dominant – but whose subfactors play out differently? That's the beauty of Path6!

On the next page you will find a "snapshot" of Richard's overall Path4/6 scores so you can see them all together. This snapshot is a one-page summary report we often use in coaching, selection, and team sessions. It displays the Path4 and Path6 graphs only and omits the text found in the full Path4 and Path6 reports. There is a duplicate of this page printed on page 188 at the back of the book also.

Summary: Path4/6 - Richard Results

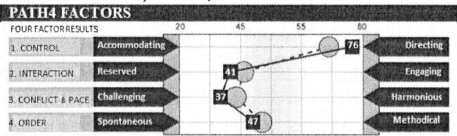

PATH4 FACTORS

FOUR FACTOR RESULTS		20	45	55	80	
1. CONTROL	Accommodating				76	Directing
2. INTERACTION	Reserved		41			Engaging
3. CONFLICT & PACE	Challenging		37			Harmonious
4. ORDER	Spontaneous			47		Methodical

⊙ Driver Blended Profile   ■ Richard Results

PATH4 FACTORS

SIX FACTOR RESULTS		20	45	55	80	
1. DOMINANCE	Compliant			64		Dominant
2. EXTROVERSION	Introverted	39				Extroverted
3. COMPASSION	Detached	26				Compassionate
4. CONSCIENTIOUSNESS	Unstructured			58		Structured
5. ADVENTUROUSNESS	Cautious				71	Adventurous
6. INNOVATION	Concrete			53		Abstract

Mid-Range

PATH6 SUBFACTORS

1.	Accommodating		66		Assertive
	Collaborative		61		Independent
	Diplomatic		52		Blunt

2.	Serious	38			Enthusiastic
	Reserved	33			Social
	Quiet		52		Verbal

3.	Logical	26			Sympathetic
	Action-Oriented	30			Supportive
	Challenging	33			Tolerant

4.	Generalist		54		Precise
	Improviser		59		Organized
	Instinctive		58		Achieving

5.	Guarded		68		Daring
	Content		66		Ambitious

6.	Experience-Based		52		Imaginative
	Practical		56		Resourceful

Jerry W. Mabe

CHAPTER 18

PATH6 – FACTOR 2
EXTROVERSION

Factor 2 –Extroversion

Introverted	Mid-Range	Extroverted

- Reserved
- Good Listener
- Serious
- Work well alone
- Modest

- Outgoing
- Talkative
- Lighthearted
- Gregarious
- Promoting

Factor 2 measures classic **Extroversion**. While Path4 measured **Interaction**, Path6 is distinct in how it measures true Introversion and Extroversion. The difference is related to *energy* in addition to communication and interaction skills as measured in Path4. An Extrovert (right-side of this continuum) is energized by being around people, engaging with them and communicating. An Introvert can often communicate well especially with people they get to know well and are close to, but too much time relating to people leaves them de-energized. They need time alone, off-line to process. As with all the factors, the piece parts of this factor are broken into three separate subfactors for each side of the trait.

The typical Struggles for both sides of the Extroversion Factor are described as follows:

Introverted Strengths:	**Extroverted Strengths:**
• Task-oriented	• Good at meeting strangers
• Serious and modest	• Lighthearted and enthusiastic
• Realistic and practical	• Optimistic
• Dry sense of humor	• Enjoys being in the spotlight
• Good at persevering	• Good at promoting
• Likes to be focused	• Likes to make a good impression
• Likes closure	• Likes open-ended situations

Refer to the diagram below which outlines the subfactors associated with the Extroversion Factor in Path6 to see how this factor is built.

Factor 2 - Extroversion

Introverted	Serious	Mid-Range		Enthusiastic	Extroverted
	Reserved			Social	
	Quiet			Verbal	

Serious: reflective, logical, practical	**Enthusiastic:** fun-loving, playful, vigorous
Reserved: self-reliant, task-oriented	**Social:** entertaining, extroverted, outgoing
Quiet: focused, succinct	**Verbal:** talkative, not reserved, loud

Introverts are often process oriented. It is not that they don't like engaging in conversation with people but relational interaction takes more energy (and time!) for these individuals. They typically prefer interaction one-on-one or in small groups of people versus crowds or large audiences. The subfactors used to further explain this score are Serious, Reserved and Quiet. Introverts are reflective, rely on logic and are realistic about potential problems on projects or assignments (Serious). They are comfortable operating on their own and prefer to focus on tasks rather than on social interaction (Reserved). Finally, they tend to be focused and succinct in their thoughts and ideas. Their replies to questions will typically be brief and to the point (Quiet).

Extroverts on the other side of this factor are people-people. They are Enthusiastic, Social and Verbal as described by their subfactors. The Extrovert is a good promoter, fun loving, vigorous, playful, and shows their emotions (Enthusiastic). They are also outgoing, entertaining and sociable. They are energized by being in contact with people (Social). You can recognize them easily as they are talkative, good with words and communicate easily and often in quantity (Verbal).

Introverted Struggles:	Extroverted Struggles:
• May appear withdrawn and aloof	• Strong need for others' approval
• Sometimes comes across as shy	• May talk too much
• Tends to be pessimistic	• Tends to be overly optimistic
• Can be curt	• May lack focus
• May appear quietly self-righteous	• May display strong emotions
• May appear skeptical or secretive	• May be too transparent
• Typically drained by social contact	• Often not good at working alone

The struggles relating to these factors are again easily identified by looking at their various subfactors. Over-done, the Introvert can be pessimistic, too serious and seen as unenthusiastic (Serious). Because social contact drains them, they may avoid face time with people and this avoidance may lead others to believe they are aloof or unfriendly (Reserved). Making small talk and meeting strangers can be stressful for the Introvert (Quiet).

For the Extroverts, when over-done become Struggles – for instance, their sunny disposition can cause them to be too optimistic and over-commit themselves and those on their team. They can make hasty decisions and miss key details (Enthusiastic). Trying to please everyone, they can struggle with timeliness, focus and setting priorities (Social).

Although they like to be heard they don't tend to listen well and can dominate conversations, not being sensitive to the needs or ideas of others (Verbal).

Let's see what Richard Results, our Case Study person, has for Path6 scores for Factor 2 - Extroversion. (See full graph on Page 159).

EXTROVERSION

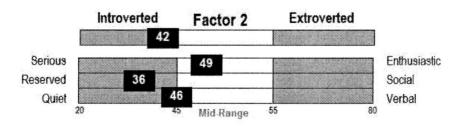

Richard is an Introvert with his score of 42 on this factor. His subfactors are Serious (49), Reserved (36) and Quiet (46). If you were to meet him you might not realize right away that he is an Introvert because he is mid-range on two of the three subfactors. He is somewhat right near the midpoint between Serious and Enthusiastic. And, he is somewhat verbal.

When engaged in a conversation about a project he is passionate about or a cause that matters to him, you will likely find that he is somewhat Enthusiastic and Verbal. However, when it comes to issues that are not of keen interest to him or when in a large group, he will tend to stay on the periphery rather than hop into the middle of a discussion.

CHAPTER 19

PATH6 – FACTOR 3
COMPASSION

Factor 3–Compassion

Detached	Mid-Range	Compassionate

- Eager
- Tough-minded
- Objective
- Questioning
- Thick-skinned
- Confronting

- Patient
- Supportive
- Sympathetic
- Understanding
- Sensitive
- Harmonious

Factor 3 measures Compassion. It is *important to note* that we are talking about natural, *behavioral* compassion not about one's values that cause them to be compassionate. A person *can* be compassionate *out of their values,* but may operate in a detached manner by natural behavioral tendency or talent. For instance, a Detached person may feel compassion for a homeless person who says he is hungry. The Detached person is naturally skeptical rather than trusting and will therefore maybe act out of compassionate values and buy the man a sandwich, but he would never likely hand him cash and assume he would use it to buy food. That's compassion acted upon out of values rather than natural behavior.

165

The motivation shows the Compassionate side of a person and the action shows the Detached behavioral side.

The left-side of this trait, Detached, is decisive and quick moving while the right-side prefers an even pace and does not take easily to change. The left-side are the head-thinkers and the right-side, the heart-thinkers. We need both.

The Strengths for both sides of the Compassion Factor are as follows:

Detached
Strengths:
- Operates well in conflict
- Objective and cool
- Action-oriented
- Responds quickly
- Challenges, makes difficult calls
- Likes change, works at fast pace
- Favors logic over feelings

Compassionate
Strengths:
- Operates best in harmony
- Compassionate and warm
- A good listener
- Patient, willing to wait
- Loyal and consistent
- Like stability, even-paced
- Favors feelings, shows empathy

Refer to the diagram below which outlines the subfactors associated with the Compassion factor in Path6 to see how this factor is constructed.

Factor 3 - Compassion

Detached	Logical	Mid-Range		Sympathetic	Compassionate
	Action-oriented			Supportive	
	Challenging			Tolerant	

Logical: solution-oriented, decisive

Action-oriented: results-oriented, goal driven, motivated

Challenging: fast paced. makes quick decisions

Sympathetic: caring, compassionate, merciful, sympathetic

Supportive: encouraging, good listener, gracious, supportive

Tolerant: agreeable, harmonious, accepting

Detached individuals are solution-oriented, hold people accountable and make difficult decisions (Logical). They tend to be very result-oriented and strive towards the goals that they or others set for them (Action-oriented). They prefer a fast pace, welcome confrontation and handle difficult situations with ease (Challenging). They remove themselves from the emotion when making decisions. Detached people are often also Dominant and/or Adventurous. They are the "take action" and "get it done" people of our society.

Compassionate people are the loyal, steady, reliable crew. They are empathetic and warm; quick to extend mercy and show care (Sympathetic). They usually enjoy encouraging and helping others, listen well and are gracious in their interactions with people (Supportive). Their patience makes them great teammates, they are forgiving of mistakes, agreeable, accepting and harmonious (Tolerant). The patience and loyalty of Compassionate people is their hallmark. They consider others' feelings and step into the emotion of situations when making decisions.

Detached	Compassionate
Struggles:	**Struggles:**
• Can be combative	• May compromise too much
• May be abrupt	• May be slow to confront
• Can be judgmental and critical	• Can be naïve and too trusting
• Sometimes too impatient	• Often resists change
• May tend toward hyperactivity	• Tends to be passive
• Prone to discontent	• May be complacent
• May appear cold-hearted	• May not verbalize true feelings

The opposite sides of this factor can have trouble understanding and relating to each other. The Detached individuals can come across as insensitive to the needs of others (Logical). In trying to get things done, the Action-oriented person may fail to listen to others and become impatient. The Detached person can become overly critical and be unbending in considering the needs of others (Challenging). They can run over people and hurt feelings in their fast-moving world, and they may not realize that the conflict they engage in for the sake of getting things done makes their Compassionate teammates very uncomfortable.

Although Compassion is a wonderful trait, Compassionate teammates have Struggles too. They can be too trusting which leads to them being taken advantage of (Sympathetic). Often it's hard for them to say, "No," which can lead to over-commitment because they don't like upsetting people. They struggle to set boundaries (Supportive). Conflict is very stressful for them and their avoidance of conflict and aversion to risk means they often do not speak up and out when they need to in various situations (Tolerant).

Let's see what Richard Results, our Case Study person, has for Path6 scores for Factor 3 – Compassion. (See full graph on Page 159).

COMPASSION

Detached	Factor 3	Compassionate

	32	

Logical	40		Sympathetic
Action-oriented	36	Mid-Range	Supportive
Challenging	25		Tolerant

20   45   55   80

Richard is clearly Detached as measured in this Factor. This is not a surprising discovery because he is so Dominant. Often these two traits are correlated and track together in direction and magnitude. His Detached Factor score is a solid left-side 32. From the subfactors we see that he is Logical (40), Action-Oriented (36) and Challenging (25). This is a man who makes quick decisions, thinks fast, moves fast and can sometimes steam roll over people if he's not careful. He doesn't get his feelings hurt easily and is not a fan of warm fuzzy words or interactions. It takes serious effort for him to understand his slower paced, more peace loving counter parts. In coaching, he likely needs to be reminded to provide positive feedback and encouragement to his more Compassionate staff members and peers. He may even do well to learn to speak to them in a slower, calmer tone than he typically uses throughout his day, especially when he is under pressure!

CHAPTER 20

PATH6 – FACTOR 4
CONSCIENTIOUSNESS

Factor 4–
Conscientiousness

Unstructured	Mid-Range	Structured

- Spontaneous
- Flexible
- Versatile
- Instinctive
- Quick
- Improvises

- Organized
- Precise
- Detailed
- Prepared
- Thorough
- Follows Rules

Factor 4 in Path6 measures Conscientiousness which deals with the need and use of structure. This is an area where people often have to learn behaviors to help them operate more flexibly or more structured at times. But under stress, duress and pressure, a person will naturally revert back and display the behavioral talents (and Struggles) related to their true hard-wired behavioral preferences.

Unstructured, the left-side of this trait, is flexible, versatile and instinctive. They are often said to "wing it" or "fly by the seat of their pants." When you ask them to change tasks, they welcome the change. They dislike sitting still for too long and are natural multi-taskers –

although they can struggle with following things through to completion.

The right-side, Structured, is controlled and pragmatic, as you would expect. They like to plan, research, organize and follow the rules. Processes and systems are their safety net and their preferred way of operating. Structured people pride themselves on being prepared and thorough. If they have a repeated action they soon create a system for it!

The Strengths for both sides of the Conscientious Factor are as follows:

Unstructured Strengths:	Structured Strengths:
▪ Flexible and versatile	▪ Organized and scheduled
▪ Works with broad concepts	▪ Accurate with details
▪ Improvises, operates without procedures	▪ Establishes systems
▪ Instinctive, operates spontaneously	▪ Prepared, rehearses carefully
▪ Makes on-the-spot decisions	▪ Analyzes before deciding
▪ Gives a reasonable estimate	▪ Conducts research to find facts
▪ Responds candidly	▪ Responds diplomatically

The subfactors associated with the Path6 factor of Conscientiousness are listed below.

Factor 4 - Conscientiousness

Unstructured	Generalist	Mid-Range		Precise	Structured
	Improviser			Organized	
	Instinctive			Tolerant	

Generalist: high level thinker, estimator, broad
Improviser: adaptable, responsive
Instinctive: informal, flexible

Precise: accurate, exact, factual, thorough
Organized: orderly, structured, scheduled, prepared
Achieving: goal-oriented, productive

Unstructured individuals are intuitive and can make broad assessments and give estimates quickly (Generalist). On the spot responses are their specialty and they improvise easily (Improviser).

Adjusting to situations and change are easy for them as they are not overly reliant on procedures (Instinctive). A change in plans is often more welcome rather than stressful for these people. They like to be on the move and are often very outgoing as well (strongly correlated to Extroversion).

Structured people are interested in details, the process, creating systems, and procedures. They pride themselves on being accurate, thorough, factual, and correct (Precise). Organization permeates every realm of their life. Open the desk drawer and you will find tidy files, look in their closet at home and it will be orderly and coordinated. They don't just make lists they follow them through to the very last item. They strive to be well prepared (Organized). Goals and milestones motivate the Structured individual; they contribute to his or her sense of productivity (Achieving). They need to know and have clarity in what is expected of them. Consider some typical Struggles for each side below.

Unstructured Struggles:	Structured Struggles:
• Not naturally organized	• Tends to be inflexible
• May 'wing it' too much	• May be too picky
• May ignore rules	• Over-rely on procedures/rules
• Can be impulsive	• Perfectionishtic to avoid mistakes
• May overlook important details	• May focus on details but miss the goal.
• May be under-prepared and over-confident	• May over-prepare but lack confidence

People who score strongly on either side of this trait can clash at times. The Unstructured person may reach a quick conclusion but miss important details (Generalist) and details *are* of the utmost importance to Structured individuals (Precise). The Unstructured person doesn't like to prepare in advance. They may lose their edge when they do prepare ahead of time as the information may be forgotten. Once it is out of sight, it is out of mind! The Unstructured person prefers to prepare on the fly or look at information right before stepping into a meeting so it is fresh. Unstructured people can jump from task to task without completing any of them, which may be seen as being unprepared (Improviser). They need accountability to stay on task to follow through to completion of their goals and deadlines – otherwise their tendency towards inconsistency may get the better of them.

If being too flexible is a fault of the Unstructured side, then being too rigid is a fault of the Structured side of this trait. Structured individuals can lose sight of the forest for counting the trees. They can become too picky and sacrifice deadlines because they are too rigid (Precise). The Structured crowd can become too inflexible and resist change. It is harder for them to improvise – even when looming deadlines demand it of them (Organized). They can become too focused on the details or goal and lose sight of their own needs and the needs of their team or even their family (Achieving). They can be willing to sacrifice all for the attainment – better yet the perfect attainment – of the goal they have set for themselves.

Let's see what Richard Results, our Case Study person, has for Path6 scores for Factor 4 - Conscientiousness. (See full graph on Page 159).

CONSCIENTOUSNESS

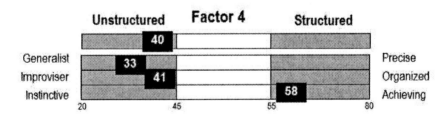

Richard is clearly Unstructured, but in this factor he is a great example of the power and importance of the Path6 tool, which allows you to look at the subfactors that compose a behavioral trait. His subfactors are *not* clustered on this factor. He is left-side Unstructured (40) with subfactors of Generalist (33), Improviser (41) and Achieveing

(58). So, let's explore what those differing scores mean.

Being Unstructured means Richard's teammates probably realize that he is a good generalist, prefers not to sit still and likes to have multiple balls in the air at one time. Because his Generalist score is the farthest subfactor from 50 for this trait, we can see that one of his greatest Struggles with relation to this factor lies in the details and precision. He probably needs to work hard at proofreading proposals and paying attention to data and specific information. His next subfactor moves closer to 50 with an Improviser score of 41. He is not naturally organized, but he probably can act in a more organized manner when forced into order. More importantly, when he is passionate about a project or assignment, he will work hard to ensure his delivery is organized. His final subfactor moves to the right-side with an Achieving score of 58. This means Richard is goal-oriented. He can exhibit more learned, structured behavior particularly when the goal or results of a project are at stake. He will have more learned behavior in these areas when he is working on something he has a passion for. If you want him to be more organized and meet deadlines then set the goal for him and tie a reward to it; just see what he can do!

Jerry W. Mabe

CHAPTER 21

PATH6 – FACTOR 5
ADVENTUROUSNESS

Factor 5 –
Adventurousness

Cautious	Mid-Range	Adventurous

- Prudent
- Minimizes Risks
- Content
- Tried and True
- Laidback
- Steady

- Daring
- Takes Risks
- Ambitious
- Pioneering
- Competitive
- Driving

Factor 5 measures Adventurousness. This is a new factor shown only in Path6 and not brought out separately in Path4. It is blended in as part of the first factor (Control) of Path4 but there are very good reasons to report the traits of Adventurousness "on its own" in Path6 because they are unique in how they play out. They are also very important in leadership development and coaching. Adventurous people do not necessarily have a high need to be in control. They enjoy challenges and risks, but they are not necessarily loners in their pursuit. Likewise,

Cautious individuals are better described as prudent and content than as compliant or accommodating. This factor describes how people assess and embrace calculated risks and challenges.

The strengths for the Adventurousness Factor's two sides are as follows:

Cautious
Strengths:
- Avoids risks
- Keeps balanced life focus
- Focuses on consensus/cooperation
- Moves cautiously into new areas
- Can be the 'voice of reason' to more daring counterparts

Adventurous
Strengths:
- Welcomes new challenges
- Not afraid of taking risks
- Sets lofty goals and strives to achieve
- Seeks challenge and adventure
- Highly motivated
- Doesn't hesitate to seize new opportunities

The Path6 subfactors associated with Adventurousness are shown in the grid below.

Factor 5- Adventurousness

| Cautious | Guarded | Mid-Range | Content | Adventurous |
| | Content | | Ambitious | |

Guarded: careful, risk averse

Content: steady, consistent, balanced

Daring: adventurous, courageous, pioneering, venturesome

Ambitious: competitive, opportunistic

Cautious individuals are prudent. They look to minimize risks they might take. They are not the great risk takers of this world, but they tend to look for potential pitfalls (Guarded) in situations and operate in a steady, consistent, balanced manner (Content). They may try to pick apart a solution just to make sure that it is sound and not too risky. If a person is Content by nature and also a good fit in their job, they won't be a great flight risk in an organization. These are the steady, consistent people in the workforce, they are slow to change positions and can be happy to stay put when they find a role that ideally suits them and is rewarding.

On the other hand, Adventurous people are daring, pioneering, venturing and like to take chances (Daring). They tend to be opportunistic and competitive (Ambitious). This trait is a hallmark of many entrepreneurs. They like calculated risks and move out boldly on those risks that they see as important. Give them a challenge and they will rise to it, and they'll look for another as soon as they have conquered this current one. Wanting to conquer something new however, you may bring to light some of their struggles such as those listed below.

Cautious
Struggles:
- Can be overly protective
- Slow to initiate
- May undervalue own talents
- May lack motivation
- Can shy away from setting personal goals

Adventurous
Struggles:
- Can be overly competitive
- Sometimes takes unnecessary risks
- May focus too much on goals/success
- Tend to think they are always right
- Want others to agree with him/her
- Can be manipulative to reach his/her goals

While Cautious people are typically great long-term employees, they can be resistant to change and miss out on opportunities because of their tendency to be overly cautious (Guarded). They sometimes need a nudge to take the leap when new opportunities present themselves. They likewise may need a nudge to accept very challenging goals. It is not so much the goal that intimidates them; it's often their natural tendency to undervalue their own talents and their slow approach to taking action (Content). They don't like to rock the boat.

As you'd expect, the Adventurous Struggles are mirror opposite to those of the Cautious crowd. Sometimes they can take unnecessary risks and choose not to see or heed dangers that lie ahead (Daring) particularly when the thrill of the chase becomes great. They are very driven individuals and may ignore others' needs in order to succeed

(Ambitious). Maintaining a work/life balance in life is often a challenge for Adventurous individuals.

Let's see what Richard Results, our Case Study person, has for Path6 scores for Factor 5 - Adventurousness. The graph of his scores on the next page reveals that he scores in the 99th percentile on this factor. (See full graph on Page 159).

ADVENTUROUSNESS

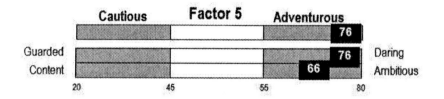

Richard is clearly Adventurous – to the max! His score of 76 is in the 99th percentile of the general population and reveals that he is even more likely to take a risk or rise to the challenge than anyone else in the room! His Daring score (76) shows that he loves a thrill and is not daunted by the need to be courageous. He is also highly Ambitious (66). From an employer's perspective these high scores translate into one key question, "Can I keep Richard challenged and motivated in this job?" This person needs to be able to feed his desire for Adventurousness so if his job were to become dull and routine, lacking in significant challenges to overcome or new heights to achieve, he will become restless. He may even become restless to the point of becoming a flight risk.

CHAPTER 22

PATH6 – FACTOR 6
INNOVATION

Factor 6–Innovation

Concrete	Mid-Range	Abstract

- Experience-based
- Realistic
- Practical
- Utilitarian
- Traditional

- Imaginative
- Original
- Inventive
- Aesthetic
- Novel

Factor 6 measures Innovation. At RightPath we believe anyone can innovate! However, the way in which we innovate varies based on behavioral wiring. This is the sixth and final Factor of Path6. This factor is not clearly identified in Path4 and thus is measured solely in the Path6 online assessment. I also believe it has some correlation to learning styles. But, since learning styles has fallen "out of favor" in the psychology community (due to validity questions), RightPath has not done correlative studies, but I think they would be interesting to pursue.

This factor measures whether individuals are "in the box" or "out of the box" thinkers. How a person comes up with solutions to problems, how they create, and how they process ideas and information

179

is measured along the continuum from Concrete on the left-side to Abstract on the right-side. The left-side represents experience-based innovators while the right-side reflects our more "out of the box" thinkers and innovators.

The Strengths for the two sides – Concrete and Abstract – for the Innovation Factor are as shown below:

Concrete Strengths:	**Abstract Strengths:**
▪ Focuses on practical solutions	▪ Gifted in abstract thinking
▪ Steady and consistent	▪ Creative, imaginative, and original
▪ Likes to deal with concrete issues	▪ Effective in coming up with new ideas
▪ Good at solving routine problems	▪ Quick minded and resourceful
▪ Practical and able to see the big picture	▪ Seeks mental challenges
▪ Sees pitfalls in an idea or course of action	▪ Able to consider an idea from many angles
▪ Finds solutions grounded in experience	▪ Good at devising new methods/approaches

Like the prior factors, Innovation has just two subfactors. They are shown on the diagram below.

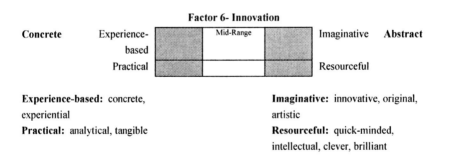

Factor 6- Innovation

Concrete — Experience-based / Practical — Mid-Range — Imaginative / Resourceful — **Abstract**

Experience-based: concrete, experiential
Practical: analytical, tangible

Imaginative: innovative, original, artistic
Resourceful: quick-minded, intellectual, clever, brilliant

Concrete individuals can and do innovate; it's just that they typically do so by experientially looking first at what has worked in the past or what works in similar situations. They are led by past experience, like to deal with concrete ideas and solve problems by looking at past solutions (Experience-Based). They are good at analyzing processes, implementing existing or slightly tweaked solutions, and they deal well with tangible ideas and issues. They like the tried and true – they create new ideas out of old ones.

Abstract innovators, on the other hand, don't like the tried and true. To them, new is better and "never before thought of" is best. They are imaginative, original, and artistic (Imaginative). The Abstract individual has an enterprising nature which comprehends theoretical ideas and develops new solutions (Resourceful). They are often academically minded and often possess an amazing capacity for retention of information.

On the Struggle side, you might see the following from either side of this trait.

Concrete Struggles:	Abstract Struggles:
▪ Relies too much on past experience	▪ May become easily bored
▪ May hesitate to act on good ideas	▪ May lack focus
▪ Relies too much on proven strategy	▪ Tend to jump from task to task
▪ May undervalue personal abilities	▪ May become impatient when others do not catch on quickly
▪ Can be slow to act	▪ Can lose momentum on follow through
	▪ May discount established methods and procedures

Concrete thinkers can sometimes rely too much on past experiences and proven strategies (Experience-based). These tendencies can mean being left behind in this fast-paced, forward-thinking world. Individuals who are Concrete can be stubborn about perspective and hesitate to act on new ideas (Practical), perhaps because the unknown in situations is not always easy to factor in to new solutions.

Abstract thinkers are often frustrated when others cannot follow their train of thought or thread of ideas. They become easily bored and can Struggle to operate within rigid sets of rules, and they labor to communicate clearly and succinctly to others as a result of their abstract thinking style. They have to learn to work on communicating clearly with and to others (Imaginative). Because they constantly hunger for "new and better," they can undervalue proven methods and become impatient with those who do not track with their ideas or catch on quickly (Resourceful).

Let's see what Richard Results, our Case Study person, has for Path6 scores for Factor 6 - Innovation. (See full graph on Page 159).

INNOVATION

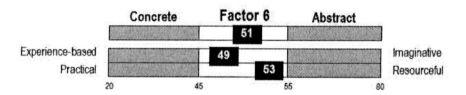

Finally, we find a trait where Richard is not extreme! Obviously we had chosen Richard Results as a case study for this book due to his extreme scores and mix of subfactors, but in this final factor he is not so extreme. His score for the Innovation factor is 51. His talents will utilize strengths from both sides of tis factor. For instance, with a Concrete (49) score he may tend to first consider past solutions that worked well when looking at a problem or challenge. He may become resourceful, however, as he tries to construct a solution for his current situation. He may tie together "tried and true" along with "fresh ideas." Richard can also appreciate input from both sides of the spectrum. He likely can track with an Abstract person's train of thought and also understand more practical, experience-based solutions as well.

CHAPTER 23

LEADERSHIP DEVELOPMENT

The age-old leadership question is, "Are leaders born or made?" RightPath says the answer is "Yes" – both! Leaders are born with some traits and a lot of their traits are "made" – more specifically, not made, but rather developed! Successful companies are led by individuals who exhibit clear and positive leadership attributes, attributes may be partially inherent, but they are largely developed. And, great leaders realize the importance of continuing to grow as they lead and cast vision for their organizations. When people are headed in the same positive direction in an organization, you will usually find that they are following a well-defined and clearly understood vision; a vision which starts at the top and is well communicated downwards. The corporate vision is well understood, people are focused, and they're meeting their goals or working to get things back on track if goals are missed.

When leaders show respect for individuals' uniqueness and differences at all levels in an organization we see that communications are open and honest. This builds trust and team unity across departments and operating units. Cooperation takes effort, it doesn't just happen. But when it flourishes, we find that morale is high even though people are working hard. Strong accountability is a final marker of stellar leadership. It is always important, but particularly critical when times are turbulent or in flux. In the organizations we work with, true accountability is the differentiator between good and great leaders.

So, how do leaders become good or better yet, great? Great leaders are open to development – and the first step of development is self-awareness. Great leaders develop themselves personally and professionally. In turn, they develop others to reach their highest potential as well. **Self-awareness and ongoing development are the hallmarks of the exceptional leaders of our times.**

Using behavioral talents as a foundation for self-awareness and development is the best place to start. Once leaders understand their talents and behavioral preferences, they can leverage their Strengths and minimize their Struggles to be operating at maximum efficiency and effectiveness. They learn the type of support they need to surround themselves with to complement (complete) them. Self-awareness also highlights the areas leaders need to stretch to make their team better. They can learn to understand the talents of those who work with and for them and help them along on their own development journeys as well. Their teams will function better, get along better, and build trust; taking performance to new levels.

Understanding yourself well and the talent you work with every day, allows you to objectively and strategically plan for the future. If your team is missing particular talents, you can be intentional to fill those gaps as openings allow. If your team is experiencing conflict or difficulty you can use behavior as a place from which to understand those challenges and resolve them quickly. It allows you to move your teams to positive, creative conflict for higher performance.

MY UNIQUE PROFILE

So, if self-awareness and development are truly the hallmark of great leaders then RightPath has devised a simple but profound place to start! This is a foundational assignment piece of every team-building session we conduct and executive coaching we engage in.

MY UNIQUE PROFILE
Step 1)

If you have completed Path4/6 online profiles then look to your two strongest scores (farthest + or − from 50) and note those two as your strongest behavioral traits. You can choose your strongest score from either your Path4 report or your Path6 report.

Strongest Traits: A) _____ Score ___

                                 B) _____ Score ___

Step 1A)

If you have not taken the profiles online, identify which two traits you believe best describe you. Circle the item most like you in each item listed below from the Path4 Factors.

Then of the four circled, marked the two that are most prevalent (strongest) in your natural talents.

Are you Compliant   or   Directing?

Are you Reserved   or   Engaging?

Are you Challenging   or   Harmonious?

Are you Spontaneous   or   Methodical?

My Estimated Strongest Traits: A) _____

                                           B) _____

Step 2)

Next, turn to the beginning of the Path4 chapters (Chapters 6 – 13) for each of your two traits, and identify the two Strengths that best describe you for each of those two traits. List them below:

Strengths:

1.

2.

3.

4.

Step 3)

Then, return to those same chapters related to your two strongest traits to identify two key Struggles for each of your strongest traits. List them below.

Struggles:

1.

2.

3.

4.

You now have recorded talents or Strengths that can help you lead well and a Struggle that you can work on developmentally. It is likely that the very things you chose as your Strengths play into your Struggle category when those Strengths are over-done. Do you see the connection (correlation)?

This is just the start. From this point you can devise an action plan to begin leveraging your Strengths and working on your Struggles. If you can identify a person who has overcome Struggles similar to yours or who naturally excels in the areas in which you wrestle, ask them for insight and help. Then come up with some specific Development Items and Best Practices to work on them.

Development Items:

Best Practices:

On the next few pages, we'll walk through an example using our Case Study person, Richard Results. See his summary graphs for Path4/6 on the next page and then his corresponding Development Plan which follows.

187

Summary: Path4/6 - Richard Results

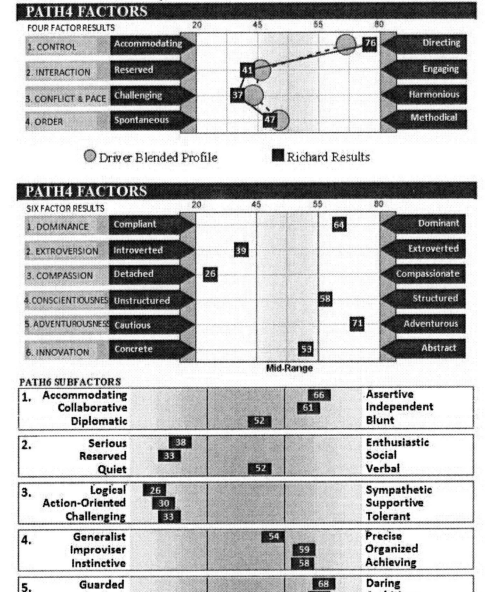

Driver Blended Profile   **Richard Results**

©2000-2013 RightPath Resources, Inc.

Richard Results Leadership Development Plan (LDP)

Strongest Traits: **Directing** = **76** (26 points from midpoint of 50)

Challenging = **37** (13 points from midpoint of 50)

Strengths:

1. Results-oriented; I meet or exceed goals that are set for my performance.

2. Moves boldly with confidence – a focused and experienced leader.

3. Does well in conflict; I am not afraid of contentious situations and push for resolution.

4. Makes difficult calls; I am often willing to make the tough calls that others will not make.

Struggles:

1. Too controlling; when I think my way is right I try to control and discount others' input.

2. Not a good listener; I am not always an attentive listener, and I tend to interrupt others while they are speaking.

3. Impatient; I can underestimate the time it takes for others to complete assigned tasks and can be impatient when processes move more slowly than I would like.

4. Judgmental, critical; I can become critical and snap at people particularly when I am under pressure or moving too quickly exhibiting poor EQ (Emotional Intelligence).

Development Items:

1. I will actively seek input from others and ensure buy-in before key decisions are made – rather than after the fact.

2. When listening, I will endeavor to ensure I am fully engaged and not jumping ahead with my own thoughts or ideas for response.

3. Before setting deadlines and milestones, I will seek input from others to be sure that the deadlines and milestones are realistic for the team members, whose contributions are needed to achieve success.

4. I will slow down and work on my EQ (Emotional Intelligence) in an effort to minimize my tendency to be critical and judgmental of others when I am under pressure.

Best Practices:
1. Before pressing forward with a new idea or initiative, I will identify key contributors and players. I will solicit their input and feedback in advance so they are not blindsided and can contribute effectively.

2. When listening, I will set my smart phone out of reach, turn off email and focus my attention on the person speaking. I will confirm back to the speaker what I hear to ensure I have captured the key details they wished to convey.

3. I will remember that others do not process information as quickly as I do. When setting deadlines, I will ask team members what their workload is like and also ask them to give me a realistic estimation for the portions of projects that require their effort.

4. Seeking to recognize my critical nature, when the pressure is on, I will make an effort to slow down. I will use effective questioning to help me slow my pace. On critical communications, I will draft email responses and wait to review them later in the day rather than typing and sending them immediately.

That's an example from our Case Study person, Richard Results. While he is fictional, the development plan is not! In fact, any person can become a leader although the leap from individual contributor to leader is not always easy. We teach people this in our sessions and coaching.

Development Helps the Move from Individual Contributor to Leader

Climbing the corporate ladder is done by working hard and reaching goals. The higher you get up that ladder, however, the more you have to learn to delegate rather than doing all the work yourself. The skills and mindset that brought success thus far will not carry leaders to the upper echelons of most organizations. Leaders doing the same thing they did to get here will not succeed. Learning to lead well often means loosening the reins of control, so the people below you can step up and handle them – freeing up the leader's time to think of the big picture.

Leaders need time to consider the future, vision, competition and other broad elements affecting the business world. Instead of being ingrained in the day to day details for the majority of their work day, they need to spend time creating vision, anticipating the future making improvements on their roles, developing their team members, as well as building relationships with their peers and upper management. To do this they must have a team working for and with them whom they can trust with the ongoing daily details and processes.

Encouragement and coaching are an integral part of leadership development. Getting results alone is not enough to build excellent leaders. As leaders move to new realms of leadership, reassurance and guidance will allow them to understand what is working well and what is not. Feedback will help them navigate through difficult times and remind them of the importance of giving feedback to those below them, as well. For the ego-driven leaders this may seem a bit contrary to the behavior that helped them reach this spot. However, the truth is that leadership can be a lonely responsibility and encouragement is the best counterbalance.

We all are leaders. Even without direct reports working for you, you lead. Other people watch you. You are a leader by influence. Your example is being noted and your influence is being exercised – even without anyone reporting to you. New teammates and current team members watch role models to learn how things are done, to examine culture, and to understand what is acceptable in the work environment. When changes are taking place, individuals look to one another for cues on how to react and act. At work, home, and in the community we all lead by example, in word and in deed.

Whether you aspire to the highest heights of leadership or simply want to make a positive impact on those you lead less formally, this process of self-discovery, self-awareness, and objectivity is the start. Understanding your talents, their Strengths and Struggles, are the cornerstone from which you can be better, do better, and lead better.

Hiring an executive coach is an excellent way to reinforce and accelerate this process. One of my CEO clients who leads a very successful global business went back for a Harvard MBA reunion. The Associate Dean (a former Fortune Executive) posed a question to the reunion group asking how many of them had an outside Executive Coach. When only about 20% of the group raised their hands, he admonished them, "Get one!" Choosing a mentor or accountability partner is good as well, particularly if formal coaching is not an option. And, don't forget to look at the leaders around you. Take note. See what they do that is worth emulating and also what is worth disassociating from. Once you are aware, you will begin noticing them everywhere – all people as leaders, their Strengths and Struggles playing out.

Take note of great leaders. Perhaps their attributes will match those that we found in the research we have conducted over the course of years with clients. Polling top leadership attributes of people's "Greatest Leaders" led to the creation of the list on the following page. This research was also used in the development of our LQ360 assessment.

Check out the list on the next page. What do you notice? Do some of the items match those you'd pick for your greatest leader? The attributes don't come from one particular behavioral trait. The Strengths are indicative of the whole spectrum of leadership talents we have discussed in this book.

Top Leadership Attributes:
- Good listener.
- Honest, trustworthy, has integrity
- Caring, concerned about me
- Straight-forward, gives clear expectations
- Motivates self and others
- Confident, positive attitude, makes work fun
- Stable, consistent, balanced, level-headed
- Trusts me to do the job, does not micromanage
- Supportive, lends a helping hand
- Respects others and me
- Fair, treats others fairly
- Sees the big picture, visionary, strategic
- Results-oriented, mission-focused, initiates, proactive
- Decisive, objective, gives direction, firm but flexible
- High standards, sets high goals for self and others, accountability

Add to that list some other often mentioned traits attributed to great leaders – like leaders who welcome feedback and who create a culture of development and coaching. The picture starts to form that good leaders are not just the ones who only get good results. In fact, the top items in that list were not results-oriented at all – they were relational. We expect good leaders to produce results. However, **great leaders** get the results and care for *and* develop their people.

There's a flipside too as we look at trends among poor leaders.
Throughout years of polling individuals in corporations and environments of all sizes, we've discovered that poor leaders also have themes or "derailers" among their leadership attributes – or lack thereof. Once again, the results come from all behavioral traits and reflect a host of Strength and Struggle tensions. Some of the chief complaints about poor leaders include:

Leadership Derailers:
- Broken trust, lack of integrity
- Placing personal agendas above those of the team/organization
- Indecisive
- Non-communicative
- Controlling, pushing own agenda
- Overly emotional
- Withdrawn
- Inconsistent

As you gain in self-awareness, use both sides of these research perspectives – great and poor leaders – to help guide your leadership development on your RightPath.

CHAPTER 24

LEADERSHIP LEGACY,
A UNIQUE APPROACH TO DEVELOPMENT

In my executive coaching practice and as the RightPath team develops our ongoing curricula, we are constantly researching and on the lookout for "what works" with our clients. We try to determine the most effective ways for leaders to accomplish the goals they are striving towards. By analyzing and searching to see what produces faster, more sustainable development for the leaders we serve in their development, we seek to bring value and solid results to both the leaders and their organizations.

In the previous chapter, we used the My Unique Profile Exercise to help you outline your Strengths and Struggles in order to formulate a plan for development. We also reviewed such a plan for our case study person, Richard Results. This exercise is a valuable part of helping individuals, leaders, and teams work on their self-awareness. The next challenge however, is how to take this awareness of self and others and move it to a development plan that creates lasting results.

A number of years ago as we built the RightPathing Your Leadership curricula to support our **LQ360°** instrument, this was on our minds. We knew we needed an "outcome-based" format for the leaders

195

we work with. Not only did we need to measure their leadership abilities in the 360° assessment, we needed to deliver that data clearly and guide the leader in producing a measurable, corresponding action plan.

Individuals who complete Path4/6 online are encouraged to understand their key strengths and struggles and use those to help them work, lead, and team better. Leaders who complete our LQ360° assessment use these more attribute-based results to formulate a Leadership Development Plan (LDP). This concept is not new. However, as we devised this plan I was very conscious of the fact that our research warned us that the biggest complaint about such plans was that once they were formulated, leaders were not exactly sure what to do with them or how to implement them.

Wanting to <u>move leaders from "data" to "development"</u> – the 360° tool's report is the output or data and the LDP is the development element. Our objective for of development was sound and the plan had been proven, but the challenge was to find a way to ensure that the information on the plan was actionable, measurable, and sustainable.

Thus, we began to ponder that perhaps the plan (LDP) was not *the* outcome after all. The more we thought about it, the more questions we asked, which led us to an important consideration. Perhaps the development plan was a step on the way to a different end goal – the *means* to an end – not the end itself? Shortly thereafter, we further considered yet another different view. What if focus on the "data"/ "development" – both plan and actions – stretched to include concentration on the element of "significance?"

We came to understand the development plan (LDP) as being a step on the road to the goal. But the most important factor for the leader being developed is to consider *"why"* he or she is developing – to grasp the significance of developing as a leader! *Significance* is the 'why' in the leadership development equation. Instead of the development plan (LDP) becoming this year's version, which will be filed away and forgotten next year, what if this year's plan became a step on the road to leadership significance? What leaders and organizations were really looking for was something that would produce change – an improvement, a shift in leadership – that could be generated and sustained.

And so, RightPath investigated what drives change, sustainable change. The first thing we considered was how organizations drive results. What drives outcomes in business? Leadership is business, serious business – in both the for-profit and in not-for-profit world that also has to steward resources. The answer was right in front of us. Everything we truly want to accomplish has a goal – an outcome! Why had no one ever looked at leaders as having a goal for their leadership? That is, a desired, stated, clear outcome for their leadership and more importantly, their leadership development. Leaders have had goals but they've had "mental" goals that hadn't been clearly articulated. The goals in the back of their minds have never been crafted into words or declared aloud. Digging deeper, we discovered one common unstated goal that most leaders have even if they can't articulate it yet – their Leadership Legacy.

First, we experimented with the concept of Leadership Legacy in our executive coaching work. We piloted the approach and technique with individuals one-on-one so we could assess their receptiveness and gather their feedback. Here's how we outlined the concept of Leadership Legacy to them:

> ### *Leadership Legacy*
>
> ---
>
> *Your Leadership Legacy is a statement you create and write out.*
> *Spend time reflecting before you put pen to paper.*
> *Ask yourself, "In your heart of hearts,*
> *what do I really want MY leadership to accomplish, create,*
> *impact, change, improve, cause, or simply 'be'?"*

One of the leaders in our pilot quickly made the connection. He said, "Oh, this is like the 'what do I want on my tombstone' or 'writing my own obituary,' right?" Backing it up a little bit from an obituary, we settled on a view of what would a leader like said about him or her at his or her retirement party. **Leadership Legacy is the PURPOSE of your leadership.**

Personally, I believe, and I tell my coaching clients that this concept has an element of "Calling" in it too. And so, I ask them also, "What do you see your Calling in leadership to be?"

As our curriculum came together, here's how the description reads for Leadership Legacy. It is a:

- A **goal** for your leadership
- An **expectation for your leadership**
- A **positive prophesy** of what your leadership is to be
- **Desired outcomes** – the impact of your leadership

With a Leadership Legacy established, my development plan is no longer the goal. My desired Leadership Legacy is the goal I am striving for and a good leadership development plan (LDP) will help me reach my goal! Having the plan is like having a map on the road to a destination, it helps you get there. And if you're in leadership, you've perhaps already had some good plans that have propelled you this far. Add to that your own Leadership Legacy and you will more clearly know where you are heading as a leader.

In our curriculum, we sum it up as follows: if Leadership Legacy is your destination, then the RightPath LQ360° (along with Path4/6) becomes your compass, and your leadership development plan (LDP) is your roadmap.

A development plan alone won't suffice; you need to know your destination or goal and that's what your Leadership Legacy becomes. Consider the old axiom – if you *don't* know where you are going, then a broken compass will work just fine and any map will do. But, if you *do* know clearly where you are going (your Leadership Legacy), and you have a really good compass (the RightPath LQ360° and/or Path4/6), and a good roadmap (your leadership development plan or LDP), then the odds go up drastically that you will get to the desired destination!

It works. The proof lies in the experience of our executive coaching clients. Furthermore, we have thousands of positive evaluations from individuals who have attended our RightPathing Your Leadership sessions where we teach this concept as part of building strong leaders and teams.

One company I work with, a Fortune 500 Company and former Fortune Magazine Most Admired Company, uses RightPath tools as part of their four-day, development-oriented, Leadership Experience Program. From our very first pilot participation in this program, the success has been remarkable. In the past, participants had indicated they disliked the previous assessment tools that they had been using as part of the program. Once our tools replaced the former tools, the rating for this segment of the program went from "worst to first." Following the pilot session, all of the subsequent evaluations indicated that our part of the program and corresponding assessment tools were highly valued and considered highlights of the program. This company is now in its third year using RightPath tools and curricula. Close to two thousand leaders will have completed our assessments as of this year. Our day of the program has remained as the top-rated day of the four-day program and participants often site Leadership Legacy as being one of the most impactful concepts learned during the program.

Authors of the best-selling business book − *The Leadership Challenge* − Kouze and Posner, released a follow-up book called, *A Leader's Legacy*. In this book, they summarize the concept of Leadership Legacy as follows:

> *"It's not how big a campfire you built, but how well you kept others warm, how well you illuminated the dark to make them feel safe and how beautiful you left the campsite for those coming next to build the next fire."*   *- Kouzes-Posner*

What would you like your Leadership Legacy to be? And, remember, you don't have to have direct reports to be a leader. We all lead at times. People on teams as individual contributors are leaders also, leading by influence rather than job title or positions. Try it! Take the time to ponder what you want *your* Leadership Legacy to be and wrestle with putting it into writing as your leadership goal. What kind of leader do you want to be remembered as?

Coach's Notes:

What would you like your Leadership Legacy to be?

CHAPTER 25

APPLICATION OF PATH6
BEHAVIOR AND ROLES –
HIRING AND SELECTION
USING BEHAVIORAL BENCHMARKS

Ask any fish and they'll tell you, it is much harder to swim upstream than downstream. When talents are well suited to and are being employed in a role, the work comes more naturally. Frustration, on the other hand is quick to surface when a role does not fit a person's natural behavioral talents and abilities. Using an example from the trait explored in both Path4/6: A Methodical or Structured person is going to feel more at home in a role that involves detail and requires structure whereas a Spontaneous or Unstructured person is going to feel most comfortable in a role where there is flexibility and mobility.

And so, many people ask what job or career would be perfect for them based on their behavioral talents. The answer is easy in broad terms. Consider your strongest behavioral talents and seek a role which puts them into play. But, in specific terms it is not so easy to predict. One must consider the economic climate, education and training, a person's passions and experience in addition to behavioral preferences.

That being said, behavioral preferences are a great place to start particularly as you look at how you can succeed in the role that you currently possess. Behavioral preferences are also a very important part of the hiring process as you look to fill positions on your team.

In some cases you may have a role with many individuals already situated in a particular position. To find the next "right fit person" for that particular role, you would be wise to look at the current top performers in that job and evaluate the ways in which those top performers are similar to one another. You can also compare the top performers to the bottom performers to see what significant differences exist in the behavioral talents of those two groups. This is called behavioral benchmarking (RightPath's form of job profiling). The success that this sort of evaluation has in the hiring process may surprise you. Consider the diagram below.

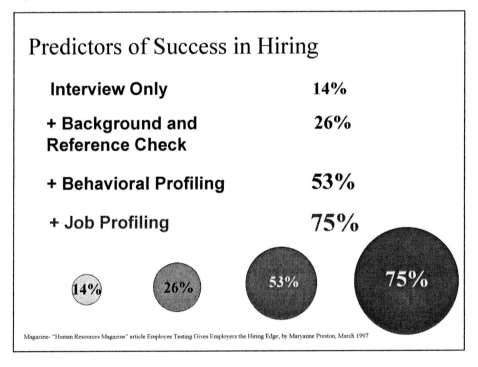

Predictors of Success in Hiring

Interview Only	**14%**
+ Background and Reference Check	**26%**
+ Behavioral Profiling	**53%**
+ Job Profiling	**75%**

Magazine- "Human Resources Magazine" article Employee Testing Gives Employers the Hiring Edge, by Maryanne Preston, March 1997

Using Path4/6 Behavioral profiles to provide the data for comparison of top and bottom performers brings a much needed element of objectivity. It is often hard for managers and even those successful in a role to specify exactly what it is that makes them successful. They may be able to tell you that high performers in a role are people-oriented for instance. But they cannot tell you at what point someone might be seen as too Engaging or chatty to succeed in that particular role. Or, they may not realize the effect of a trade-off between a person's Engaging talents and their ability to work with detailed procedures in a particular role.

Once you have a clear idea of the commonality between the top performers in a role, you can then employ behavior-based interviewing in your hiring process. Because you know which factors and subfactors matter for the role, you can assess to see how candidates compare on those elements. This is typically done after the first few rounds of interviewing and hiring investigations. Candidates who make it through the initial interviews and whose background and experience match the role may then be asked to take online profiles.

While an employer should never hire or fire based solely on any one source – including behavioral assessments – they can use the assessments as an indication of a person's behavioral talents. Assessments are also a good foundation from which to ask interview questions. We never want RightPath tools used as a thumbs up or thumbs down hiring tool. We want our profiles to be a great tool in a great manager's hiring tool kit. For example, if a person needs to exhibit attention to detail for a particular role and their scores on the fourth Factor (Order and Conscientiousness) are mid-range scores then you can ask behavioral interview questions about their attentiveness to details, organizational strategies and goal orientation to see if they are indeed a fit for the role. Likewise, if a different person scores in the high sixties in Factor 4, you will want to ask them behavioral interview questions about any tendency they might have to overanalyze things. Or you could ask when they have struggled with performance because they couldn't move from research to resolution on a project. This is what we call behavioral interviewing.

RightPath has crafted a set of behavioral interview questions that our clients use. We also help them to create their own behavioral questions. By utilizing behavioral interviewing, the hiring manager asks questions intentionally to confirm that a person's demonstrated behavior matches your expectations, based on their profile scores. They also ask questions to interview for the gaps. That is, if a person's scores are not strong enough to indicate a desired strength in a particular area of talent then ask questions to see if the individual being interviewed has learned skills to help them in that particular area of talent.

The high predictability of behavior allows this process to work incredibly well. We have created benchmarks for customer call centers, sales positions, customer service roles, real estate, human resources positions, and retail store managers.

Consider the power of benchmarking. One of our recent clients shared that he had been using a RightPath benchmark and behavioral interviewing questions in twelve nationwide locations. Over the course of one year, he has experienced a 26% drop (on average) in turnover for the role. Two of those twelve locations reduced turnover by 40% and one location by 50%!

For more information on RightPath's benchmarking process for selection, visit our website at www.rightpath.com and select the Team tab in the main menu for a segment on Hiring and Selection.

CHAPTER 26

PATH4/6 PROFILES FOR YOU AND YOUR TEAM

RightPath Behavioral Profiles, Path4 and Path6, are easy to complete online. Reports are available immediately and can be printed as well as saved electronically. We invite you to try them out!

A discounted rate (20%) of $75 is available for purchasing profiles for you and your team. Visit www.rightpath.com/site choose "Take Profiles," "Buy Path 4-6," and "I have a promotional code to use for my purchase." Enter the promotion code DYDT when prompted.

More information on RightPath Resources, Inc. our assessments and our services can be found on our home page – www.rightpath.com.

SPECIFIC RESOURCES:

RightPath offers a host of curricula suited to you and your team. Some of our Path4/6 based sessions include: Teaming for Success, Mastering Creative Conflict, and Leadership Balance. To find out more about these and other sessions visit the curricula section of our website at http://www.rightpath.com/site/info/curricula/ .

If succession planning is your area of interest, **Leadership Continuity** is RightPath's approach to succession planning. By studying what was not working as organizations tried to plan for succession, we came up with a strategy for Leadership Continuity that really has proven successful at all levels of the organization. Read more about this process at www.rightpath.com/site/individualsandteams/leadershipcontinuity1 .

Other assessments available from RightPath include the RightPath LQ360° assessment, and RightPathing Your Future (whole-life career planning suite of assessments). You can learn more about these products at www.rightpath.com/site/assessments/ .

A WORD ABOUT VALIDATION:
RightPath Path4/6 Behavioral Assessments
- Based on our experience in 13 years of use, we estimate the tools show a 90% accuracy rate which, for a 25 minute assessment, is impressive
- Clients in post-course evaluations across industry spectrums (including many Fortune 500 companies) have recorded a 95% accuracy rate since the tools' creation in 1999
- Independent IO Psychologist development team provided external psychometric validation along with construct and content validation
- Assessments were cross- validated against other highly regarded psychological instruments
- Third party validation using spouse or significant other was completed on large sample
- Test-retest validity (stability over time) show exceptional results. With a coefficient of 1 being no change at all, the RP tools had a .86 test retest validity

RightPath LQ360 Leadership Multi-Rater Assessment
- This tool has research validation along with psychometric validation of the EQ (Emotional Intelligence) modules.

For more extensive validation information call RightPath Resources, Inc. at 877 843 7284.

APPENDIX

FAITH-BASED LEADERSHIP

I could not write my first book about RightPath without including a section on Faith-Based Leadership. By this I mean how I believe our faith impacts our leadership.

First, I'd like you to know why we chose to name our company RightPath. To me, the name is best embodied in one of my favorite Bible verses, Proverbs 3:5-6.

Trust in the LORD with all your heart and lean not on your own understanding; in all your ways acknowledge him, and he will make your paths straight.

In one contemporary translation of this verse, the last segment of it reads as, "He shall lead you on right paths."

I believe we each have God-given gifts, gifts that impact how we lead. These gifts are what I believe our Path4 and Path6 profiles measure and explain. We call these "hard wired, natural behaviors" because they are innate – not temporary or learned. And, when I am speaking or teaching personally rather than in a corporate setting, I am quick to explain that if we measure "wiring" then the description includes the connotation that Someone must have "wired" us the way we are – rather than it occurring randomly. I believe very strongly that each of us is "wired" very intentionally. Perhaps stated better, I don't ascribe to a "Big Bang" behavioral theory.

Path4 and Path6 show you and measure the way you were "woven" just as David speaks of in Psalms 139:13, "For you created my inmost being; you knit me together in my mother's womb." (NIV) Psalms is one of my favorite books in the Bible and I particularly like a contemporary translation which says, "I am intricately and wonderfully woven." (Psalm 139:14) As leaders we are "intricately and wonderfully woven," and I believe that 'Weaver' is our Creator, God.

How we use these God-given gifts – that are woven into our very being – directly impacts our individual leadership. It allows us, as leaders, to impact other people, organizations, our community, and the world around us. I believe that how we use our God-given gifts also correlates to the achievement of our ultimate purpose in this life. I believe the ultimate purpose for all of mankind is to "enjoy God and glorify Him forever." God – the same God who spoke the world into being – uses His limitless creativity in amazing ways as we fulfill that purpose.

How does this relate to our leadership development? How does it affect the way we coach leaders? How best can we develop others and teach them to keep growing and developing and to bless those they lead by helping them to do the same? Let me explain my perspective. Understanding our own individual gifts and how they are woven into our "wiring" allows us to accept and understand the natural strengths of those gifts. When we relax in the knowledge that we are not going to be perfect, nor is any other human being going to be perfect, then the pressure to try to be perfect is lifted. And when we acknowledge that along with our Strengths we will also have some Struggles – by design – then the fear and uncertainty diminish. Instead of trying to decide what Strengths to play to or succumbing to pressures that may not fit the way we are wired, we can instead look at what is predictable, based on our wiring. We can understand the gifts, their accompanying Strengths, and their related Struggles and see that they are very predictable in our leadership and behavior. And, predictability is not meant to pigeon-hole you, but rather to free you to exercise those strengths, anticipate those Struggles, and employ your leadership gifts most effectively.

The book, *Good to Great*, researched organizations and exceptional leaders. In great organizations, they found leaders who embodied a *paradoxical* blend of personal humility and drive for the organization. The paradox of these traits is a good place from which to explain why understanding our natural leadership wiring is so crucial.

These exceptional leaders are *paradoxical.* A paradox is, by definition, a seemingly self-contradictory statement or proposition that in reality expresses a truth. Personal humility and drive for the organization are paradoxical. In fact, with all the Path4 and Path6 behavioral assessments we have administered and through years of executive coaching, we can attest to the fact that it is extremely rare to find a leader who is *naturally wired* to have *both* drive for the organization *and* personal humility. From our study of behavior, we have learned that the leader who is *naturally* wired for strong drive will usually struggle with having (and showing) humility. Leaders wired for drive and who do possess humility also have typically *learned* humility and worked to develop it over time. Equally so, the leader who is *naturally* wired to possess and display sincere humility will usually struggle with having (and showing) drive. A humble leader who is also driven has usually learned to tap into that drive and has worked on developing it over time.

Bringing your faith into your leadership is one thing. Learning to rely on your faith, as a leader, goes a step beyond. In fact, bringing faith into your leadership is, in my opinion, the best and most sustainable way to develop your leadership. It is faith that allows the unnatural part of exceptional leadership the opportunity to flourish alongside your natural gifting. Why? Because you aren't doing all the work yourself. Faith brings a supernatural force to your leadership that allows you to operate out of the boundaries of your normal wiring. What is uncomfortable for you becomes more natural when manifested by the inner force of faith. The more you practice walking your leadership role in faith, the greater possibility it will be sustained. Permanence becomes the mark of positive leadership improvements because the change comes from within rather than from external pressures.

Do I think you have to have a personal faith to be the sort of leader Jim Collins speaks of in *Good to Great*? As your friend I'd ask you to ask that very question – of yourself - rather than of me. Why? Because how you answer that question will have personal impact for you that reaches far beyond your leadership.

As you begin to contemplate your answer, let me tell you that the greatest improvements I have ever experienced with leaders who have made huge strides in leadership development have involved us bringing faith into our coaching relationship. As the leaders have done this, their leadership has been stepped up like never before and the results have been both remarkable and sustained over time.

What side of the paradox do you fall on? Are you naturally wired to have drive for your organization or are you naturally wired for humility? Have you tried working on your non-strength side on your own? If so, how did you fare and for how long? I contend that if you think about these questions you may very well find that an additional source of power to develop the non-natural side for you would surely be welcome especially if you've ever worn yourself out trying to do it solo.

The questions aren't done however. Faith is a vague term to some of us. Find a quiet place and ask What, or Who, has the power to help you learn and grow in this manner? Where is your own personal faith best rooted? As I leave you to ponder these challenging questions, I also offer these words from Jeremiah 29:12-14(NIV).

"You will seek me and find me when you seek me with all your heart. I will be found by you," declares the LORD, "and will bring you back

from captivity."

Finally, if you would like a little more information from a pastoral perspective, I have included a few recommendations. These pastors are leaders who lead well and exemplify the principles I have just explained. These individuals represent three generations who walk the talk. Randy Pope is lead teacher and pastor at Perimeter Church in John's Creek, Georgia – where I make my church home. Andy Stanley, is lead pastor at North Point Community Church – a church that has significant global influence. And, Bart Garrett is lead pastor at Christ Church East Bay in Berkeley, California – a place where academia, culture, and spiritual life collide for God's purposes.

If you'd like to learn more about these pastors, their churches, and leadership teams, you can find them at: www.perimeter.org, www.northpoint.org, and www.christchurcheastbay.org .

These sites offer a wide variety of messages. In some cases you can search by topic such as leadership or the workplace or family. Furthermore, as a helping hand, I have taken the initiative to select a few messages on leadership from each of these men that you may find insightful. See below for these resources:

1) The book entitled *The Intentional Church* by Randy Pope and the book *Insourcing* also written by Pastor Randy Pope of Perimeter Church.

2) "Leading Great" by Andy Stanley of North Point Community Church - http://northpoint.org/messages/follow/leading-great/ .

3) "Vocare – The Life of Moses" - three messages entitled Called, Crafted and Captured by Bart Garrett, Christ Church East Bay www.christchurcheastbay.org/Christ/Resources/li/Vocare__The_ Life_of_Moses/ .

Jerry W. Mabe

ABOUT THE AUTHOR

Jerry Mabe is the founding CEO and president of RightPath Resources, Inc., a leadership and talent development company. RightPath has a vision and "Calling" for leading individuals and organization to align people, passions and positions to achieve maximum performance. RightPath Resources® provides leadership and talent solutions, utilizing a proprietary internet-deployed suite of assessments measuring hard-wired, natural behavior (Path4/6), career development, EQ (emotional intelligence), and key leadership attributes (RightPath LQ360⁰). RightPath also provides consulting services in leadership development and assessment, hiring, teambuilding, career development, Leadership Continuity (succession planning), family businesses and executive coaching.

Clients include executive level individuals and teams at many Fortune 500 and Fortune 1000 companies, multiple NFL teams' leadership, medical/health care related businesses and high net worth entrepreneurial families and their businesses. RightPath solutions are also being taught in various universities, MBA/business schools and seminaries in the United States. Major clients include Southern Company, Clorox, State Farm, TSYS, Weather Channel, Scripps Institute (Fortune's Top Health Care Leadership), Regions Bank, Atlanta Falcons, McKesson, State Farm Insurance, The John Maxwell Company, SF49'ers, Goodwill Industries and many others.

Jerry brings a unique blend of his own diverse personal experience as a Fortune 500/1000 executive and corporate officer. He is a successful entrepreneur with a passion for "Calling" to his work with his clients.

Jerry serves as a senior executive consultant, session facilitator, coach and a keynote speaker at conferences, various professional associations and universities around the U.S. His personal work areas (and speaking topics) include using behavior and assessments in executive coaching, leadership, EQ (Emotional Intelligence), family businesses, team building, career development, benchmarking, Leadership Continuity and selection. He has taught many of these topics in visiting faculty roles at partnering universities.

Previously, he was co-owner and senior vice president of A One Service Personnel for 10 years. (This company was acquired in 1995 by Select

Appointments, PLC - an international staffing consortium based in London, England.) Prior to its acquisition, this Atlanta-based full-service staffing company had grown into a three-branch operation, including an accounting specialty division, providing jobs to over 3000 people per year. Services included retained searches, placements; out-source project management, testing and assessments, temp-to-hire, and temporary placements as well as succession planning. A One Service Personnel used assessment extensively in its services which led Jerry to build RightPath after the staffing company was acquired.

Before joining the staffing venture, Jerry built over 16 years senior executive leadership experience in various corporate officer and executive leadership roles in marketing, national sales and operations positions as an executive for two Fortune 500's and a Fortune 1000.

Jerry is a Tar Heel native of Winston-Salem, North Carolina, and a graduate of the University of North Carolina at Chapel Hill with a B. S. degree in Industrial Relations with a focus in psychology.

He resides in Cumming GA (Atlanta area) with his wife, the former Penny Gaultney. They have two children, Micah, age 21 and Joy, age 19. They are members of Perimeter Church, where Jerry serves as an Elder. He and Penny are directors of their First Harvest Foundation and are also members of the North Georgia Emmaus Community. They are also active in other mission and philanthropic endeavors.

Jerry's favorite activities center around family time at their second home at Lake Chatuge, North Carolina, along with jet skiing, snorkeling, wine collecting, Tar Heel basketball and teaching on his passion, Calling.